Surviving a House Full of Whispers

Sharon Wallace

Library of Congress Cataloging-in-Publication Data

Wallace, Sharon.
  Surviving a house full of whispers / by Sharon Wallace.
      p. cm.
  Includes index.
  ISBN-13: 978-1-932690-90-3 (trade paper : alk. paper)
  ISBN-10: 1-932690-90-5 (trade paper : alk. paper)
  1. Wallace, Sharon. 2. Adult child sexual abuse victims--Great
Britain--Biography. 3. Child sexual abuse--Great Britain. 4.
Abused teenagers--Great Britain--Biography. I. Title.
  HV6570.4.G7W35 2009
  362.76'4092--dc22
  [B]
                                            2009010720

Distributed by: Ingram Book Group, New Leaf Distributing,
Betrams Books

Published by **Modern History Press,** an imprint of
Loving Healing Press   www.ModernHistoryPress.com
5145 Pontiac Trail   info@LHPress.com
Ann Arbor, MI 48105   Tollfree 888-761-6268 (USA/CAN)
USA   Fax 734-663-6861

Table of Contents

Index of Poems

Integrity and pride

I carried a heavy load and wore it with dignity,
Never ceasing to believe the Lord would rescue me
On my lowest days of living, when I wanted to scream and shout
I prayed the Lord would save my soul from the here and now.
I asked him daily to forgive my sins and cleanse me in the lake of crowns
To place his hands upon my head and lift me to his throne.

"Where are you Lord? Answer me," were the words I used to say
He never uttered a single word, But I knew he heard me pray

I carried emotions inside my mind sometimes wanted to die
In my bleakest hours I felt alone as family watched me cry
Months turned to years, the hurt did subside,
And life became good again
But I will always remember the night of that dream,
When I heard the good Lord say

"Be still my child, I will wash you clean,
But not from committing a sin.
But to wash off the hands that burdened you that night
And made you want to give in
I heard your calls and your prayers, each and every one

I sat beside you, holding your hand, when this terrible deed was done.

I always rocked you gently and walked a little behind,

For you had the strength and wisdom, you knew how to survive"

"Where are you, Lord? Answer me," were the words I used to say

He never uttered a single word, but now I know he's never far away

1   Bitter Sixteen

Breathless from running! I was thankful night had thrown a dark blanket across the city because it enabled me to scurry unseen down the cobbled streets of Devon like a night creature. I slipped into the house quietly and unnoticed; raking my fingers through my tangled hair and wiping the remainder of dried blood from my arms and legs with the cuff of my cardigan, which I had wetted with spit. I knew it was useless to tell anyone about my stepfather—or even of my escape from him just a few hours before.

Everyone had been convinced that I was a liar; he had managed to fool so many. I lay on my bed with solitude as my only friend and fell into the abyss of loneliness, unsure if I wanted to go on with my miserable existence any longer. The song "walking in the rain" by the Partridge family echoed through my head. The verse "Oh how much I need someone to call my very own"! Repeatedly sprang through me until I thought I would go insane.

How had this happened? I was sixteen and it was the summer of 1973. In a few months, I would be seventeen yet I was scared to walk the streets of my own town. I scanned the walls of the bedroom that I shared with two others and their one-eyed Granny. The double bed slept all three of us girls and Granny had the single bed in the corner. I know this family had put themselves out to accommodate a very mixed-up teenager. But I thought they were kin after Lynda, their daughter, had married my brother Mark. The bedding was cleaner than ours at home and topped up with old army coats when the weather got colder.

Although a poorer home materialistically, it was more inviting and if I closed my eyes for a second, I could pretend this was my life and my past had never taken place. I believed if I were good and kind to fellow man then I would reap the prize God gave for this selfless action. I also believed sticking to the truth was the right path to choose. Wrongdoers will never prosper.

I thought about Mother and home and realized it was Saturday; she would be cooking the evening's banquet. It had been two days since a morsel had touched my lips; my appetite had ceased for six days—my cravings diminished. Normally when Mother starved me for more than a few days, the pains in my belly stabbed and twisted unbearably as the aromas emanating from the kitchen permeated my every pore. But now I couldn't even think about food—this current pain was too intense. Even the money I had managed to save did not spur me to buy rations.

The one-shilling I had hidden in my sock had been there since my interview with the police, I needed to know I had something in an emergency.

We were never poor or without food in the cupboard, unlike many others. Unemployment was rife and holes in your shoes and clothes was something everyone had and quite normal. Stepfather was a good shoplifter and his daily raids on the local shops were unique. An offender uncaught in many ways, he even stole joints of meat. It was still an era when you could leave your backdoor open without fear of burglars or assault and all kids played in the streets. You also knew the names of every house and were friends with everyone from your area.

Our favorite games were hopscotch, hide-and-go-seek, and skipping rope. Two balls bounced off a wall and caught in unison was another favorite of mine; I even managed to juggle five balls at once. I was always the best at everything and needed to accomplish this in all I undertook. Cherry knocking was the most daring game I played (*knocking on doors and running like hell*) the buzz and euphoria I felt whilst running away from my courageous acts of rebellion made me forget the horrors of home for a few minutes. For that hour or minute spent outside the home I was Sharon—the mutinous one the girl who emitted the character of bravery. If my friends could see how I cowered in my house of whispers, I believed they would suppose I deserved it for allowing it to continue. I should have had a childhood that was easy and untroubled and filled with days of lazing on the curbs doodling with stones and making dens in the nearby woods

If I had any doubts about being alone, the unmistakable truth was now confirmed. I buried my head deep into the pillow while my mind whirled in chaos. I could hear the faint sound of a television program drifting up from the family room downstairs and I tried to distract myself from feelings of desolation. I went to the window and saw the isolation of night outside hiding the world's injustice while my reflection stared with troubled eyes back at me.

"Just you and I, kid."

I must never show weakness again was the conclusion reached during my reverie.

Early on Monday morning I made my way to the bus stop. Social Services were going to help me, whether they wanted to or not. I dreaded showing my face on the streets again—he had terrified me this time and I knew he would be looking for me and would eventually catch me, but my determination to survive was apparently greater than my fear. I wished I could erase the last six years and go back to being Sharon Arscott, the orphan. I preferred to endure the stares of compassion from people's eyes to the glares of condemnation that they now cast on me.

I had nothing to lose as I boarded the city bus and climbed to the upper deck. I slouched in the back seat and defiantly lit a cigarette as the bus passed the bottom of the road where my mother lived. I studied people who came and went and wondered what their home lives were like, but the ringing of the bell and the conductor loudly announcing that the bus had arrived at my stop released me from the prison of my envy and deep contemplations. I gathered myself to do battle before walking—with attitude—toward the Social Services building. I entered and wondered to myself what they would do for me and why no one from this department had offered me a home in foster care. I was uneducated about such things, but I knew my life could not continue this way. I was terrified about my future and even more anxious my stepfather would get to me before I could escape to a safer place. Stepfather was right about one thing, he could commit murder and bury me beneath the soil to rot with no one to miss me, or mourn my passing. I shuddered as images of his face once more invaded my thoughts.

"I want to speak to a social worker."

"Who is your social worker?"

"I don't know—my last one died."

"Take a seat." Unfazed "I'll see if someone is available."

My manner was abrupt and I was prepared to fight and defend myself against anyone who dared to judge me wrongly or deny me anything. I waited for what felt like hours until an older lady appeared in front of me. Her tweed skirt fell around her petite frame and her brown flat shoes shining as though they were made from glass. Her hair neat and her makeup exact, like the person I had imagined my grandmother resembling.

"What can I do for you?"

"I need somewhere to live and I think Social Services should help me."

"It's not that simple young lady; you can't just walk in off the street and demand a home."

"Don't patronize me! I am homeless because I trusted people like you and now I need somewhere to live! You can't leave me on the bloody streets!"

"With that attitude young lady, no one will help you. Now let's start again, shall we?"

"I don't give a damn as long as you help me." I felt liberated knowing I could say and do exactly as I pleased because no one could physically hurt me but, as she led me into a small room, I panicked a little when it suddenly occurred to me that they might try to lock me away. I gave my name and a summary of past events when asked. Then she left to locate my paperwork, promising to return shortly.

I lit a cigarette, slumped back into the chair and tried to act comfortable with my attitude yet feeling a little guilty about how I was behaving toward others. I looked around the room and noticed its bareness.

Thick tobacco stains darkened the color of the walls and the stale smell of the room was just as dense. A large oak table stole the attention as it mastered the room with its ambiance and I noticed that pamphlets had been placed on it in neat rows. I arrogantly decided to scatter them across the room and watched as they floated across the heavily stained floor. I dragged a chair to the window, but my malice was interrupted by the return of the lady carrying a file.

"I see you have problems at home. Is there any way you can return?"

"No, I can't go back there—he will kill me."

"Have you tried to apologize to your mom?"

What? "Apologize for what?" My voice started to become louder.

"Oh I see, you still maintain it happened. Where are you living now?"

I tried to cooperate as best I could but her scathing remark about apologizing to Mother was reverberating in my mind like a crazed raging bull. My control slipped and my inner child tried to come forward, thinking she could defend and protect me.

Many people don't understand a child's desperation or their reactions to having a childhood being stolen from them. Growing up in a dysfunctional family does not necessarily mean you know how to handle it or protect yourself. Nor does being manipulated make you an expert on defending yourself against manipulation

A single teardrop fell as the small child inside me tried to claw her way out from deep within my soul searching for a breach in the unbreakable, impenetrable exterior I had worked so hard to build. I turned my face and quickly wiped away any trace of her existence and convinced myself that my composure was regained as my stomach lurched with memories of the night devil holding me down and touching me; his demonic, laughing face forever etched on the backs of my eyelids. An endless nightmare of abuse that had begun when I was just nine years old. He was a large-framed man with a round face and stood six feet and a few inches in his bare feet. Stepfather had been in the navy and I believe he was a stoker or so Mother had implied. The tops of his arms were thicker than my waist, or so I believed.

This morning's mug of tea surged to be expelled as I felt his hands touching my skin; my numb mind unable to erase the ugly memory. I managed to push down my simmering emotions and hide them from the judgmental eyes of the old bag talking to me.

My inner child was once more forcibly repressed, and replaced by the ugly bitch that could cope with all evil heaped upon her.

"I don't think there is much we can do to help you."

"I am not bloody leaving until you *DO* help me! I am under Social Service's care until I am eighteen and you bastards screwed up my life the day you returned me to that hellhole!" I screamed with a determination and rage I had never felt before. I rose from my chair and kicked it against the wall. I wanted to physically attack this woman; I thought I was losing my mind. Anger seared through me and my head felt as though it would burst and project my flesh, blood, hair, brain-matter and skull-shards in a grisly gore. I ran from the room, slamming the door behind me and kicking the walls in the lobby. This new surge of anger frightened me and thoughts of physically attacking another person scared me more.

"Stop that! If you continue, we *will* call the police!" the receptionist threatened.

"Do I look bloody scared? I don't think so!" I shot back with venomous hostility before returning to the interview room. The lady was gathering the paperwork but had dropped them as I entered—she was visibly shaken. The sight of her obvious fear she had forced me to calm myself. I wasn't comfortable causing fear in anyone. I stooped to help her pick up the dropped papers, hoping to get past this moment as if it never happened.

"Look, all I need is a little help." I begged. "I have nowhere to go."

"I'll see what we can do but our resources are limited. Let me make a few phone calls," she offered in response.

After she left, the silence in the room was comforting; I could hear the ticking of the wall clock and the muffled sounds of people talking from the offices on the other sides of the walls. The faint clicking of typewriters and the ringing of the bell as each line was finished turned into a musical tempo. My eyes were heavy from lack of sleep. I balanced the chair on two legs against the wall as the droning voices began to soften my mood and the now relaxed atmosphere began to soothe my agitated soul. I was the most relaxed I had felt in a long time, cocooning myself into my little world.

Noise from the traffic outside became hypnotic as my mind drifted back in time, remembering a car journey from the past. I was four years old and starting a new life. Meeting my brothers for the first time likened to the unknown future I faced again now.

The slamming door made me jump as the social worker returned.

"Did I startle you?" No apology offered.

I coughed nervously and replied adamantly, "No, I don't scare easily."

"Would you consider working at a holiday camp? It would solve the problem of accommodation and earning."

I agreed immediately without asking a single question.

"You start tomorrow. The owner is doing this as a favor to me so you won't even need an interview. I will issue you with a travel warrant and also a little cash to tide you over until payday."

The social worker felt it necessary to add that others had tried to help me but apparently, in her opinion, I was my own worst enemy. To her and the rest of the world I was nothing but a mixed-up teenager, a troublemaker, and a problem that she did not know how to solve. They knew me as the accuser—not the survivor. She said I was not making it easy for myself, and my attitude toward anyone in authority was totally obnoxious. Yes, I had deep-rooted revulsion and anger toward social services and the police because no one believed me or helped me the way a victim of abuse—*or any child in need*—should have been helped. I was never rescued. I wonder how they would have reacted if they had to live a week in my shoes; would they even survive or would they simply die in an invisible heap of expendable, unworthy life as they expected me to do?

I returned to the waiting area and the receptionist kept a keen eye on me. I was excited about the possibilities that lay ahead and frightened by the unknown at the same time. I would miss Mark and June but knew in my soul that they had both already turned on me. June was angry that I could say these things about her Dad. I understood her reasons and actually felt guilty for hurting her. Mark never believed me either and had started to get verbally abusive toward me although he too had been a victim of the never-ending onslaught of physical abuse our stepfather dished out to all.

Stories were being created and circulated about me and boys: I was a misfit and a liar; a whore that slept with everyone. Someone even thought it necessary to report to Social Services that I was a liar and that I was extremely bossy within my 'house of whispers'. I wished some of it were true! Maybe then I could have fought my abusive stepfather and defended myself. I thought *if only people put in as much effort to help me as they did to try to dismiss and destroy me, I would be fine.* My behavior was said to be absurd at times; aggressive, rude, nonconformist—and that I hated everyone and everything around me. I loathed my stepfather with a detestation that was consuming my soul. My mother hated me because of *him*. How was I supposed to react? What is the proper protocol of behavior when you're being abused? What is the socially correct way to treat your abusers?

"There you are Sharon; I hope you make the most of this fresh start." She handed the warrant and one-pound cash to me. I was given the ferry schedule and location and told I would be leaving tomorrow. I boarded the bus to return to Pam's house, looking at every landmark along the way and trying to take in as much of the scenery as possible, burning the images into my mind, my heart aching as loneliness engulfed me again.

I entered Mark's mother-in-law's home and found him and Pam sitting in the kitchen; each looking to the other uneasily. I knew Pam wanted me to leave and it felt like I had walked in on a conversation about me.

"Don't worry. I'm leaving." I sarcastically informed the two.

"Who cares? You have done enough damage always scrounging off others!" Mark viciously shouted after me as I climbed the stairs to pack.

Other children are 'raised' by their families; mine considered me a homeless inconvenience that scrounged necessities of food, shelter and safety from them. Things they apparently possessed precious limited quantities of, with none to spare for a little sister or daughter.

"Dad says you are nothing but an evil liar, you bitch!"

His ravings hurt me deeply; he knew better than anyone about what really went on in that house. He suffered terribly from our tormentor—just as much as I did. I was shocked to hear Mark's words of revulsion hurled at me. "Don't ever address that asshole as dad again! He is *Taff!* He has never been and never will be a father!" I screamed back. (Taff was—and still is his nickname.) Pam remained silent as a verbal battle raged between brother and sister.

That was the last time we spoke. I heard the back-door slam and looked out of the window in time to watch as Mark headed toward mother's house. I knew I could never hate him, but I felt immense anger toward him for treating me this way. I desperately wanted to call him back to tell him how much I was going to miss him; he had been my big brother for so long. I needed one person to say they believed me, just one set of arms around me to cradle the ache and I longed for the comfort of another human to tell me that I was lovable and valuable. The only person who had shown me a little compassion was June, but I felt uneasy in her presence. I loved my little sister very much, and missed her, but she refused to believe that her father was a monster toward me so my little sister was no longer my sister.

"Paul, where are you?" I wondered how he would react toward me. Would he turn his back on me and punish me for speaking out too? I was starting to forget what he looked like. I remember the blond hair and his ears that protruded so far out of the side of his head he was ordered by the navy to have an operation to pin them back. Mine were also protruding and Mother mercifully never allowed me to forget. Flaps—big ears— spiteful words that had a terrible effect on my ability to function properly when swimming. My biggest fear was getting my hair wet and my ears sticking out like mug handles. My tears fell silently as I thought about my brothers, who were once my heroes. We were a trio for so many years while growing up in the various children's homes. My sadness was a heavy load to carry and it started dragging me down. I shut down my mind once more to the emotions surfacing from within. My heart felt like it would burst and shatter with all the pain I was choking back. Death had not parted us, so why did I feel so bereft?

I left the house early the following morning, slipping out quietly to walk the streets of my youth for the last time. My ferry was scheduled to leave at nine o'clock and the social worker had said she would meet me at the terminal. I believed she was doing this to make sure I left so she could finally be rid of me. I was clearly a complication no one wanted to handle. I settled on the quayside hoping Mark would come and say goodbye. But how could he? I had left without telling anyone my destination.

The social worker arrived and yammered on about this being a wonderful second chance for me and advised that I not blow this opportunity with my temper, then wished me well. As I boarded the ferry, my heart grew cold and sad as intense feelings of rejection engulfed me like a shroud. It was true; there was no one to hug, no one to miss me and no one waiting for my return. How did I become so abandoned, dejected and alone? The sun was warm that beautiful June day but an icy-bitter snowstorm raged in my heart as the ferry chugged away from my past and toward my future. I watched the shoreline until it disappeared and stood facing the wind to hide my tears. I could feel a mask of resistance cover me.

I was astonished at how short the journey was; it had taken only thirty minutes to reach my destination. Standing on the quayside, I realized I was in control finally and had made these past few decisions on my own. The dense mist that had enveloped me for many months was finally being burned off by the sunshine and I no longer felt I was being clamped in the jaws of a beast; putting distance between the monster and me had helped a lot.

A young woman approached and asked if I were Sharon. "I'm Judy, one of the entertainers at the camp. They sent me to pick you up." I was thankful to see her as I was feeling a little lost and bewildered with my strange new surroundings. She remarked about my age and thought I was brave to leave home so young on my own. *If only she knew the truth,* I thought.

It truly was a new life for me. No one knew me; no one knew of my recent experiences. For the first time, I was just another teenager working my way around the UK.

I was shown to my caravan immediately upon our arrival at the camp. It was explained that normally everyone shared the vans but I was a late arrival and the other staff members had been accommodated weeks before, therefore, I would be alone. For me it was a nightmare, not a blessing. I would have freely and eagerly swapped with anyone who asked. Each night I would check under the beds and each wardrobe. I was terrified the night devil was hiding in the van, waiting to attack me again. I always made my bed a certain way and if it were touched while I was gone, I would know. It was a ritual that had started to become an obsession. My job was to clean the other vans on site and help in the kitchens. I received no news from home.

I could not trust anyone and found it hard to make friends. I started to lie about my past and steal food from the kitchens to gorge on in the evenings. If someone asked questions about my family, I invented stories of a close-knit household. My nights were lonely, yet I laughed when a joke was told and gave the impression I was happy, confident and knowing, but the Sharon who lived alone in her van at night was a frightened child who slept fully clothed, never used the communal shower and used a bucket to pee in, rather than walk into the night to the toilet block.

I would hide in my van during my days off while the rest of the staff went to their homes and returned to their families for a few days. I was often asked how my time at home went but I could only lie and tell them about my Dad's house because there was nothing else I could offer. Dad owned horses and chickens and missed me terribly when I was at work. It was a fantasy life and one I would even convince myself was true.

I longed for Father-Arscott to rescue me from this dreadfully lonely existence and I wanted the night devil to admit to the inexcusable things he had done to me. I was still naive and unworldly and desperately wanted mother to know the truth—I believed we could have a normal mother and daughter relationship one day.

"Where are you going when you finish here?" Sally asked. Time was fast approaching when the site would close for the winter; I had no idea what I would do and had not yet considered this problem.

"I am not too sure, what about you?" I deflected.

"I was raised in an orphanage so I suppose I may try getting on a winter cruise ship."

This surprised me because Sally was always so positive. I wanted to share the truth about myself with her but was afraid it would be used against me; I trusted no one. Another woman, who was much older than myself invited me to travel with her on the open road. I considered other options.

I scoured the papers for vacant situations and one advertisement caught my eye—a nanny was needed in Peterborough. No experience needed. A phone number was listed so I called later that afternoon and was asked to attend an interview in Devon, only a few streets from my parent's home. I agreed but was unsure whether I would attend. After a lot of soul-searching, I decided to chance going back; the probability of meeting anyone would be insignificant because it would only take a few hours.

This time, I boarded the train for the journey back and as it neared my destination, I felt as though I were walking back into the jaws of the beast. With each mile, the sun became cloudier, the day darker. I stood in the carriage as the train entered the station. Although the station was announced over the loud speaker I still leaned over the platform to check as the train slowed—an old habit. The sign on the platform displayed the name of the station. *Plymouth.* I wanted to scream! Breathing became difficult, panic made me lightheaded and dizzy. I collapsed back into my seat; my legs had become two strands of overcooked spaghetti. A young man asked if I were OK.

"Yes thanks. The train jerked," I lied.

"Do you need help getting off?"

"Um, no, I am all right."

He left me sitting on the seat and I tried to control my breathing. I needed to force myself to leave the relative safety of the train. I wish I had returned on the ferry at least the distance of the quay were further away from Mothers. Standing on the familiar platform conjured the ghosts and demons of my past with a force far too close to reality.

I scurried to the nearby taxi stand and fell into the first cab available. After telling the driver where I needed to go, I sat back and watched as we passed the familiar avenues.

When we reached my destination, I quickly scanned the street and ascertained that it was empty and safe. I paid the driver then rushed into the garden of the house and urgently knocked on the front door. I stated that I was there for my interview and resisted the urge to look over my shoulder again. The door opened wider and I was invited in by a woman who was clearly the granny. Her grey hair was neatly scrapped into a bun on her head. Her tiny frame held her neat attire and her slippers a bundle of fluff. The epitome of what I always deemed a grandmother would look like. She ushered me into the lounge offering me a cup of tea which I gracefully declined. I wished I had belonged to this gentle serene old lady that stood before me.

I looked around the lounge; it was a tidy home with many photographs of small children and the atmosphere was warm and friendly. After answering all the questions, I was informed that I would find out if I had the position later that evening.

"Phone me about nine this evening dear and I'll let you know."

Stepping into the street, I wished I could stay in this peaceful house forever and fantasized that I was leaving only to go to school and would return in a few hours. I longed to see my brother but dreaded his rejection. Suddenly, as I walked toward the bus stop, I spotted my sister June in the distance with a few of her friends. I quickly hid from sight behind some greenery and waited for them to pass. I felt as though I had died and now was watching life go on without me—I *could not* be seen.

I walked away slowly, glancing back only once to watch as she disappeared over the hill. When I arrived back at the train station, I felt relieved to be leaving but also a little smug because I had been walking the streets and no one had seen me.

I phoned that evening and was informed that the job was mine. I was expected the following week and my train ticket would be waiting at the station for me to pick up. I was an excited and apprehensive sixteen-and-a-half year old kid who was now employed to look after someone else's children—me, this mixed-up teenager who was barely able to cope with her own life.

I almost skipped to my van that night, proud of what I had accomplished for myself. When I opened the door, I noticed instantly that my bedding had been ruffled and I was sure someone had been in my van. I searched it frantically, thoroughly, but couldn't find anything—yet my sixth-sense was in alarm mode and telling me I was in danger! I looked out my window, scanning the darkness, and saw the night devil himself! Horror took hold as I crashed backward, landing on the floor; my fall broken by my elbow and shoulder. Stepfather was outside my van looking at me. He waved when I tried to peek through the curtains. Paralyzed with fear, I held vigil and waited with a kitchen knife in my hand until dawn broke. My radio was the only noise to break the silence of my small tin tomb. Bob Dylan's "Knocking On Heaven's Door" was swirling through the air.

In the morning, I rushed to the office to phone the police but no one believed me. *Perhaps it was my imagination*, they offered—but it seemed so real. The police suggested that maybe going back had sparked my fears and my imagination. I convinced myself they were right and my stepfather had no way of knowing where I was. I was afraid I was losing my mind. *If I were hallucinating this, would I be believed about the past seven years?* But for the next few days, strange things continued to happen. I believed I was losing my mind. People didn't seem to understand that the effects of being abused sometimes only starts after the abuse has stopped. I was too embroiled in my survival and afraid to show any emotional scaring for fear of the confrontation. It's only when I left my prison did I relax enough to react to my pain.

This was the first time I made myself physically sick and as the contents of my stomach hurled from me, I felt relief and excitement as I watched it fall forcefully into the bucket. I felt liberated and in control. I did not know then that mother had gone to Social Services demanding to know where I was. She then had passed the information to Stepfather. Luckily, no one was aware that I was leaving in a few days and my address and destination were known only to me.

Letter to My Demon

Standing alone with only my thoughts haunting my brain—the knife starts to hurt

A slice at a time peeling it thin—my skin raw as the bleeding begins

I need to get clean cut the dirt away and watch the horrors flow from my veins

Once the blood runs, I can feel the relief of the terror and shame that's being unleashed.

Masks are for faces—gloves for hands—hats for the head and scarf's wrap around

Knifes are for taking all the hurt away—I want to be free can't live this way.

Cutting the core of the evil that's been done I wear the long shirts so no one will judge.

Wounds to remind me—seen by a few—but the ones in my head are seen only by you.

2 New Beginnings

I settled into my new job. It was a challenge to work with children not much younger than myself—two boys and a girl. Allison and George, my employers, both worked long hours. Allison was about the same age as mother but very trendy, I envied her the strength she showed and the ability to be the best parent I had come across. George was a meek, quiet man who just seemed to be there whenever you turned around. A man of few words but a good provider. I was also surprised by the size of the house. It was a small three-bedroom home and I was to share a bedroom with their daughter.

Allison asked if I planned to be going home for Christmas and my mind raced to find an answer. I promised instead to let them know later that week. Nothing more was mentioned and my seventeenth birthday came and went without fanfare or anyone knowing. Its uneventful passing was nothing new to me because I was not accustomed to having celebrations to mark the passage of another year—no one else cared.

Christmas was fast approaching and the bustle of the preparations soon began. My eating habits were all over the place as food became my obsession and took over my daily routine. I felt smug when I could drive out a meal, but soon, I could not control it. I could eat three packets of biscuits, four chocolate bars, a full plate of roast potatoes and a side of fries, consuming all in one sitting until I felt my gut would burst. Knowing the thrill of being sick lay ahead gave me excitement and contentment. I knew it was wrong and that I had problems, but I could keep it secret which only complicated my addiction and fuelled the thrill.

"Would you like to stay with us for Christmas?"

I was surprised but gratefully accepted the invitation. I had been living there for about 10 weeks and was starting to relax more in their company.

"What about your family? You never phone anyone and nobody ever phones you. I have not noticed you writing to anyone either, nor do you receive any mail."

I blushed with humiliation. How could I tell them the truth? How could I tell them that I was rejected by everyone who knew me and cast aside like a used tissue? My family refused to believe me, choosing instead to believe a lying, child-abusing pervert. Therefore I could not trust that anyone else would ever believe me either. I was fed up with trying to convince others that I was not the lying, ungrateful bitch that my family portrayed me as. I decided to compromise and offered only that I was raised in a children's home and had no one. I felt awful about lying but the truth was too painful and embarrassing. I wanted to leave the pain and memories in Devon.

For the first time in years, I was looking forward to Christmas. I bought the family presents and was thrilled as I wrapped them—giving the gifts felt wonderful. Christmas morning arrived with an atmosphere of excitement, invoking memories of distant Christmases in Wales.

Everyone exchanged gifts with one another and even I had been given a few to open. Their kindness to include me in their family Christmas celebrations overwhelmed me and made me very emotional. Excusing myself, I disappeared to my bedroom, overcome with emotion. The hard exterior I portrayed on the outside was again precariously close to cracking.

Allison appeared in my room, "Are you alright? You seem upset."

"Yes, I'm fine—just a little tired. I'll be down in a minute." I kept my back toward her to hide my real, sad and vulnerable self.

She returned to her family downstairs and my thoughts wandered off on their own to home, and my brothers. I speculated what each was doing and knew June would be fine, the floor of my parent's home would be covered with gifts for her. Making my way to rejoin the family, I sat on the stairs and listened for a while as the excited squeals from the children echoed.

"This is what it should be like. What did I do that was so bad? How could I have changed it?" I wiped the tears, gathered my composure and returned to the lounge.

Christmas went quickly and New Year's Eve arrived. Again, I was invited to stay and share in the celebrations with the family. As midnight approached, I decided to phone Mark. Dialing the number for the fourth time, I held my breath, this time allowing it to ring. Mark answered the phone.

"Hello... Hello! Who's there?"

I listened to his voice and heard loud music in the background and realized he was having a party. I could not find the courage to speak; Mark got impatient with the silence and put the receiver down. That was enough for me. Just hearing his voice, I knew he was fine so I decided to go to bed just before Big Ben chimed in the year of 1974. Snuggling into the blankets, I tried to convince myself all would be fine.

I was attracting the attention of Andrew, the son of Allison's friend. He was twenty, from a wealthy family and studying to attain a degree in electronics at University. I was seventeen with no family who cared about me, and with no prospects of improving my life, but we seemed to hit it off anyways. We went out together on a few dates but I avoided being alone with him. I didn't know why I felt afraid but I did.

Our relationship was destined for failure and Allison seemed angry with me after I had yet another fight with Andrew, who wanted to take the relationship further.

"He really liked you Sharon. You have broken his heart! What's the matter with you?"

"I'm not ready to take a relationship as far as he wanted to go." I felt embarrassed with the conversation and wanted to tell her to, fuck off and to mind her own business! My anger bubbled just below the surface.

"You go on with that attitude and you will be left on the shelf; a sour old maid." This was a side of her that I had never seen and her words were spiteful. Allison's attitude toward me had changed. It started with, "Can I pay you next week? I have no money," to a month going past with no wages. Allison had guessed I was alone and had nowhere to go when she was fishing for information before Christmas. I had mistakenly thought she cared about me. She thought she could treat me however she pleased.

I didn't object for fear of being homeless, but the rage I felt toward her propelled my decisions to make changes. No one in this house really knew the real me and the thoughts that raced around my head, fuelled by anger, frightened me at times. I fantasized killing another human (usually Taff, my stepfather) regularly. I started to skip the housework and hated doing the smallest of jobs. I was being used, and my vulnerability became a weapon used against me. I needed to get away soon—the rage I felt was destroying my life!

Without Allison or George knowing, I searched for another job and was offered a position in Bishops Stortford. Getting my train fare was trickier; I stole the money from Allison's purse and left a note that read: "Fuck you! You still owe me two months of wages!"

I made friends easier in Bishops Stortford and was amazed by the accommodation offered. I had my own shower and felt secure, and could continue my eating disorder undetected. I became regimented with it. I was the only employee living on the premises and my job was to look after the children and housework. The eldest daughter was sixteen, only a few months younger than me.

I had not been in touch with anyone from Devon for a long time. I was becoming stronger in mind, more aggressive toward others and outspoken. It had now been eight months since I left and I convinced myself that I no longer cared. I met Terri, a local girl who was from a similar background. Terri wanted to be a lad and dressed that way but I couldn't help liking her. In 1974, gay people were shunned, a taboo subject and cross-dressing was hidden from the public's eye. I started to drink heavily on my nights off and when I was drunk, my anger would spill over and I deliberately tried to antagonize people into verbal confrontations. My journey to self-destruction was well underway.

One evening after another drunken session, Terri and I decided to walk to the park nearby. We were on the swings being a little too boisterous and were asked by another girl to keep our noise down. An argument ensued between Terri and the girl and I tried to defuse the situation but the girl hit me in the face and caused my nose to bleed. I was shocked for a few seconds and wanted to run away, but my old pal *anger* rose and *made me* strike her back with such force that she fell to the ground.

Terri laughed and I turned to walk away, but the girl's boyfriend had different ideas. He grabbed me and pinned both my arms down. I head-butted him, forcing him to release his grip and I then beat him about the face and head while also kicking at him. I was crazed and out of control. Hearing his girlfriend scream returned me to my senses. I was horrified by the sight before me, by what I had done, and ran off as fast as I could, followed by Terri who was laughing and shouting obscenities at the couple. After exhausting myself from running, I flopped down on the grass and held my head in my hands.

"Jesus Christ! What have I just done? I could have killed him! I wanted to keep hitting him." I lit a cigarette to calm my nerves.

"You just taught him a lesson and it will be a long time before he attacks a girl again. You bloody well surprised me!" Terri screamed excitedly as she slumped to the grass beside me, exhausted too.

I acted cocky and mimicked his girlfriend's screams, reenacting the scene continually, but inside I felt sick to my stomach, my hands trembled with adrenalin.

"Come on! Let's go to the river. The police are probably looking for us and they won't think to look there," Terri suggested.

We sat on the riverbank and I gazed into the water at my reflection. How I could hurt another like that was beyond my comprehension and I was filled with guilt and shame because of my actions. "Oh, bloody hell; don't look up, we have company!"

I looked in the direction Terri was looking and saw two police officers approaching.

"Oh shit! Run!" Terri shouted as she headed off in the opposite direction. I jumped to my feet and tried to follow but the officers were quickly upon me. They grabbed my arms and I started to struggle; I hated being held down and unable to defend myself.

One landed in the river and the other lost his temper with me and started to wrestle me to the ground. Confused and frightened by his actions, I started to lash back. My strength was frightening as I escaped their grip—no one was going to hurt me again and forcing me to the ground invoked feelings of rage and hopelessness, triggering a surge of self-protecting adrenalin. Pulling hard on the officer's hair, I reflexively kneed him in the groin and his grip on me relaxed immediately.

I ran blindly, slipping often on the grassy bank. When I turned briefly, I saw the officer who had fallen into the river now standing over his colleague, dripping wet, trying to assist him off the ground. I made my way to the safety of the woods only stopping to rest when my lungs felt as if they would burst.

The trees stood tall around me and the scrub was thick enough for me to hide in. I tried to make sense of it all. My mind tells me one thing—my heart says another. I took no pleasure from the events that had just taken place, although the rage still coursed through my veins. How do I get rid of such anger, such hatred, and such self-loathing? Emotions inside made me feel worse and the guilt from these feelings were confusing, consuming and damning to my self-worth.

This was a small community where everyone knew each other. I swung between feelings of elation and guilt, while acknowledging that I was *now* finally able to defend and protect myself. I realized; I had won against the boy in the park and the officers—the night devil wasn't going to know what hit him if he ever came looking for me! I was finally starting to relax when I heard the snapping of a twig. The daylight was fading fast. Carefully, quietly, I looked behind a few trees toward the noise. I was stunned to see at least six police officers scouring the woods and I knew they were looking for me. I was determined that I would not go without a fight. One of the officers shouted, "There she is!"

I had been spotted. I started to run but they caught me. I was too exhausted to fight despite my determination but I think in truth, now that I realized that I could defend myself when I needed to, I no longer felt so determined to fight this unimportant battle. The police were not going to beat and rape me. I was arrested for assault and my boss was informed. She came to the station to tell me I was no longer needed.

"You were crappy employers anyway!" I screamed as she left the room.

In the morning, I was released without charge. I was angry with myself as I made my way to Terri's home. I related the night's events, trying to give the impression that I was tough and didn't care, but inside I was dying. Again I was without a home, only this time I was responsible. Again, I demanded Social Service's help. I explained my history and reminded them that they were responsible for me until I turned eighteen.

They placed me with a local fanatical religious family. My behavior was appalling! I cared about, and for, no one and I drank myself stupid when alcohol was available. Making myself sick after each meal was the only thing I found pleasure in. Depression swept over me and suffocated me with feelings of self-harm which constantly invaded my mind. Holding the knife close, I considered the idea of cutting my flesh, hoping to release the hurt that was knotted tightly within my stomach but I chickened out of cutting myself. I headed toward the toilet and once more expelled my food instead. I didn't like the person I was becoming but was powerless to change; my inner thoughts did not reflect my outer attitude.

The family I was placed with did regular séances and I had walked into the house a few times while they were trying to exorcise demons from others. It was one of the weirdest homes I had stayed in but I felt no fear from their activities or of the visitors who screamed in strange voices as others chanted away the demons within.

"Christ Shaz! I wouldn't stay here with all the spooks—you never know who you're bloody talking to!" Terri mocked.

"It's the living you have to be afraid of, Terri; they're the ones who will hurt us."

Arriving back from the local shops I noticed the social worker standing at my front door. I panicked! Was I going to be moved? However, the truth of her visit was worse; what she said rocked my world to the core! Mark had been looking for me and he wanted me to phone him.

I started to shout and swear at her. "I told you not to tell anyone where I was!" Inside, I was secretly happy that someone cared enough to even look for me, (besides the night devil) but I always displayed the opposite. I was afraid to show my real feelings—I guarded against being defenseless or appearing needy.

The social worker was quick in defense, saying,

"No one has told him where you are. He asked about you at Devon Social Services and they passed the message on to me. He will be phoning my office tomorrow at three and it's up to you if you want to speak to him," she snapped.

I wondered for the rest of the day and all that sleepless night about what my brother wanted and secretly hoped he was going to tell me Mother wanted me home—that the night devil had confessed everything.

The next day I hesitated outside the office. I lit a cigarette to calm my nerves and sat for the longest time in contemplation of what I would say as I scratched at my arms until they bled. I had begun to attempt to release the night devil's poison from my body by scratching; as the blood oozed, I felt my body release the toxins left from the night devil's horrid touch. I covered my new wound and flicked the cigarette into the street before entering, ready with my rehearsed speech.

"Hello Sharon, I am glad you came. Your brother seems very eager to speak to you."

I smiled as politely as I could. The phone shrilled loudly and made me jump—my mouth was dry and my legs shook uncontrollably—my nerves strung tight.

"Hello Mark. Yes, she's here." She passed the phone to me. I held it to my ear, lost for words and nervous about why he was calling me.

"Hello, how are you doing?" Mark inquired.

"I'm doing really well. I have a job and I live with a good family. What can I do for you, why have you phoned?" I turned cold and distrusting without warning. I could kick myself for my antagonism but our last conversation was of harsh words and I could not forget that easily.

"Why don't you come home? I really miss you."

"What for? No one wants me and besides, I have nowhere to live."

"You can live with Lynda and me. We have a son." Mark sounded sincere and very mature. "I would love for you to meet him. Do you have a phone number where I can reach you?"

"I will have to think about things, Mark. I'm not sure that I want to live there." I started to get suspicious—this didn't *feel* right. "Ring me at this same number tomorrow at three. I'll let you know then."

"Sharon, listen to me. If it doesn't work out, you can always leave again. You will be there tomorrow won't you?" He sounded almost desperate. *I wish I knew why things felt so funny, so wrong.*

"Yes, I'll be here. I need to think about this. Bye." I dropped the receiver and stared out of the window. This was bizarre; I had just spoken to Mark and he was asking me to come home.

The conversation did upset me. I had missed him so much but had managed to bury my feelings toward him and the past deep inside.

"I bet you feel better after talking to your brother," the social worker prompted, trying to elicit a response.

"Not really. You will never know how much this has turned my life upside down, but hell—none of you believe me, so what's the point in talking to you? He's phoning tomorrow at same time. Is that all right?"

"Yes. Fine. But think carefully though and don't cut off your nose to spite your face."

Patronizing old bag, I wanted to scream.

"You have to have a face to cut your nose off. In my 'house of whispers,' I was faceless."

I suppose if any of them admitted that they believed me, they then would have to admit they did not do their job. I was very rude to the social worker and was unable to understand why I could not respect anyone. I said no when I meant yes and vice versa. The one thing I was sure of was the rage within that was like volcanic lava waiting to erupt. I felt as though I were an electric kettle that never reached the whistling stage.

I tossed and turned for another night, trying to decide. *Did I really want to put myself through it all again? What would happen once Stepfather knew I was back?* Maybe the passing of time had healed my mother's anger. I still craved mother's love and longed for her arms around me. I wanted to belong and be a daughter she was proud of and loved. Maybe the night devil is sorry and will apologize, maybe he will try to make things right. *Maybe...* Even these feelings made me feel immense guilt. I knew people would judge me for wanting to return to the very home all my birthday and Christmases wishes had been trashed and to the night devil's lair. But equally if I lost all hope of ever being loved by mother I believed I would curl up and die. You see I was returning as an injured party full of hope that Stepfather would tell the truth. Not as the liar and shameful arrogant bitch everyone believed I was.

I decided to take a chance and return to Devon. This time I was not alone, Mark being nice to me was the deciding factor. Saying farewell to Terri was harder than I expected. I was going to miss this mixed-up teenager who believed she was a boy trapped in a woman's body. She had been someone I could count on.

"I am really going to miss you, you're my only friend and you understand me better than anyone."

"I'm going to miss you too, but this is something I have to do."

"What the hell did they do to you?" Terri asked, almost hysterical.

"What do you mean? No one has done anything to me."

"It doesn't matter. Be happy Sharon." Terri knew she had hit a raw nerve.

"You too; and stop the bloody drinking," I laughed as I playfully teased. Now there were two friends in my life who will always own a piece of my heart—Molly and Terri.

Again I boarded the train, returning to the abysmal people I had fought hard to leave. As the train pulled out of the station, I stood at the door leaning out of the window waving until Terri could no longer be seen. Sinking into my seat for the long journey home, I gazed out the window and thought about Molly, wondering where she was and what had happened to her; was she happy?

I loved the scenery and the ways the countryside changed with each bend in the track, and wished my life were simpler. I thought about Mark and the reasons for our lack of communication. Tears welled in my eyes as I remembered my siblings and our adventures in Plymouth. If anything, our lives had been simpler then. I tried to remember what Paul looked like and tried to envision his life now; I truly missed my big brother. I pushed my emotions back and reminded myself to "never show weakness."

I decided not to show anyone, not even Mark, just how happy and excited I was to see them. Mark and June were there to greet me as I stepped off the train and as we hugged each other, I could feel the emotions rising. I shoved them deep down again. Nothing was said about the reasons behind my leaving and I was thankful because I was not sure if I could talk to June about it—after all, her biological father was my night devil and I felt immense guilt about causing her pain. She was the one good thing to come out of the union between my mother and him.

Mark explained that we were to go to Pam's house, as tea was made and waiting for us there. I was a little uneasy and nervous about the possibility of bumping into the night devil, but the time had come for me to face the animal and publicly denounce him as a liar and child abuser. I prepared myself to face his anger—I was not going to be bullied and chased by him for the rest of my life!

As we walked into Pam's home, it was as though I had never left. I wanted to turn around and run as images of the night devil instantly flashed through my mind, memories of the pain and torture he inflicted upon me rushing forward all at once. I don't know who I was trying to kid with my "I don't give a damn attitude" the truth was I was scared witless.

"You will be staying here for a while," Mark announced casually.

I looked at Mark in total disbelief of what he had just said. Memories flashed back from last year—scenes of Mark cruelly locking me out of his home on some nights, of making me sleep in his outside toilet when his rage erupted. I knew I did not want to go back to living like that. I had forgotten so much that had happened and had walked around and existed by ignoring what I saw. The truth was I was never happy in Devon and my family had been incredibly cruel to me, including Mark. *What was I doing back here?*

"You told me I was to stay at your home!" I was furious. "You got me back here under false pretenses!" I had not returned to Devon to live with Pam—had I known, I would *never* have returned. I trusted Mark and had left the relative safety and comfort of the little corner of England where I had chosen to live. I now had no money to return but I was not the same person who had left this city last year, and tomorrow I would leave again.

I found another job working locally as a nanny and never realized how easy it was to get work of this nature. Once again, I settled in with a new family; Thomas and Susie were my new employers. They had two small children and the house a little bigger than the last. I was happy and became comfortable just visiting with Mark. My dreams, haunted by fear, were back in full force. I ached to see Mother again but knew she hated me and any chance of a mother-daughter relationship with her was nothing more than a pipe dream.

One day I was asked to take the children to town and buy them shoes. I agreed, secretly happy to get out of the house, even with the children. I had never looked after children this young before—Jack was three, he had a mop of shocking black hair and the deepest blue eyes I had ever seen and the baby Lucy only seven months old. It was hard work on me and sometimes I felt stressed by their constant demands; they needed to be kept amused every minute of the day. The baby's cries sometimes cut right through me and provoked feelings of rage in me toward her attention-seeking demands. I had thought that all babies were sweet and gentle, like Molly Dolly.

Oh, my Molly Dolly. How I missed her and my past, before the 'house of whispers'. Thomas offered me a lift in the car and I gratefully accepted. It had been a month since I settled in with this family and I felt worthy and content, although my weight had ballooned as gorging on food had taken control of my life. I had mostly quit drinking because I dreaded being inebriated and found by the night devil; I needed to be constantly aware and alert.

Since returning to Devon, my eating habits had spiraled into a daily routine of gorging and puking. My depression had deepened and self-harm was always in the forefront of my daily activities. I had been working hard daily to keep the house clean and the children amused and cared for and I deserved this break from routine. This was my first day in town and I wanted to enjoy it and take my time.

Thomas literally dropped me off in the town center and sped off before I could assemble the pram. You needed an engineering degree or something to accomplish such a complicated task, especially while balancing a toddler precariously from under one arm. I had to place the baby on the pavement—it was quite the struggle—until a kind lady stopped to help.

Bloody hell! How the hell am I going to master the bus on the way home! I wondered. "Come on Jack, and keep up!" I called to the little guy, his short legs running to keep up with my rather fast and larger strides. I had so much to learn about little people. After buying their shoes, I realized that walking with a little guy in tow was better achieved by a slow crawl. We finally seemed to be working in harmony; little Lucy was fast asleep snuggled up cozy in her pram. I remembered when I was fourteen and babysat for a neighbor, I would make the baby cry so I could comfort her. Guilt coursed through me as I tried to understand why; thankfully I knew I would never do this to these two little people. *Maybe I just needed to feel needed, who knows?*

"Would you like to have some dinner, Jack? Shall we go and have some yummy fries?"

The little guy eagerly agreed. The first hurdle was to maneuver the pram through the door of the diner, then to bounce it over each step, which shook the baby like a rattle. I ordered the fries and sat back in my chair, totally exhausted by the Olympic size hurdles I had just mastered. Lighting a very much-needed cigarette, I slowly started to relax as Jack made a pie from the sauce and sugar left on the table.

"I am never having kids Jack; you little people are too much like hard work."

Jack chuckled as he squeezed the tomato sauce out onto the table, dipping his finger and relishing the taste. I sensed someone watching me and scanned the room quickly. I didn't notice anyone I knew but this uneasy feeling of being watched was very strong. The meal arrived and little Jack ate his fries with gusto. I sipped a mug of tea and stole a chip from Jack's plate and dipped it into the sauce. The feeling of being watched did not go away and as I looked around, searching for the cause, I noticed an older lady.

Who the hell is she staring at? I wondered, disturbed about being looked at.

As I turned away to check on Jack it suddenly dawned on me who the lady was—Mother! Gathering the children, I fled toward the stairs in absolute panic. Jack was crying—he wanted his fries and his crying agitated me. I picked him up and shouted for him to stop crying.

"Would you like some help with the pram?" a helpful stranger inquired.

"Yes, please! Shut up, Jack, please! I'll get you some more fries," I shouted as the man looked on shocked. I left the café and made as much distance as I could between Mother and myself before I would dare stop to calm Jack. The poor little guy was running to keep up with me, frightened about what was happening and not knowing why. I finally stopped to catch my breath and realized how bewildered he was.

"Come here, little man. Shaz is sorry," I ruffled his hair. "How's about I buy Jack an ice cream?" The look on Jack's face told me this would make up for the way I had just treated him. At home, I was relieved to see that Jack had forgotten the day's events and not spilled the whole story to his mom and dad. I decided then not to go back into town and was very upset that I had not recognized my mother—and that I reacted the way I had.

As time passed, I found it easier to cope with the children. This was the best home I had worked in despite that I had been awakened by raised voices on more than a few nights after I had retired for the evening. Thomas and Susie had started to argue regularly and things were tense at times. I tried to stay out of the way.

One morning, Susie asked, "I would like you to be home for six o'clock this evening. Thomas and I would like to discuss something with you. Can you make that time?"

"I suppose. Am I going to like what you have to say?" I added jokingly, uneasily. I was worried maybe Jack had told them about the adventures he had in town.

If they were going to dismiss me, then I would tell them to stick their job anyway, I decided. The day went by slowly; the anticipation of the evening's discussion was torture. By the time six o'clock came, I was ready to fight—and wound up as tight as a coil. I entered the kitchen prepared to use the speech I had rehearsed all day.

"Thanks for making time, Sharon. Thomas and I have something to say and a proposition for you."

"What proposition? Have I done something wrong?"

"Not at all silly," Thomas interrupted. "In fact, we are delighted with you and Jack adores you. Susie and I have been having problems and we have decided to live separately but we still want you to stay and look after the children."

"Oh!" I was relieved and took a deep breath. "I will stay—if my hours stay the same and I still live in," I added.

"Yes, of course. I wouldn't have it any other way. But there is another little problem, well not a problem but it's a bit unusual."

"Now I'm intrigued. You have my attention," I joked, finally relaxing.

"I am staying, Susie is the one leaving. Will you feel comfortable with this?"

"Why should I not be?" I asked defensively.

"Oh, no particular reason," Suzie answered. "It's just that Thomas thought you may not like the idea of staying in a house alone with a man, that's all."

"You don't bite do you? I don't have a problem with that," I lied. I went to my room and lay on my bed, thinking, for hours. Of course, I had a problem with it. A bloody big problem, but I was not about to show my defenseless side. *Never show weakness.* I knew these feelings were irrational but I could not rationalize them.

Susie left the following week. The children seemed fine and unaffected by the change, but I was a wreck. At night when Thomas came home from work, I went straight to my room and locked the door and wedged a chair under the handle. I started making my bed in that special way; my eating habits changed, eating everything in sight but without making myself sick and gaining weight rapidly. During the day, I would munch away on crisps and chocolate bars and hoard food in my room to gorge on at night. I avoided all unnecessary conversation with Thomas and never made eye contact. This went on for weeks. I was an emotional wreck and decided I needed to look for another job.

I couldn't face telling Thomas that I was leaving so I sneaked out of the house one night after dark, feeling unable to live a minute longer under the same roof.

Tomorrow Is Not a Given Day

Tomorrow is not a given day
But one we should never portray
For when wrong is done in yesterday
Tomorrows can help yesterday's stain

Forever in our thoughts memories that glow
Yesterday can start to make tomorrows sow
Tears of happy thoughts and prayers
Watching children who know we care

Tomorrow is not a given day
But one we should never portray
For when wrong is done in yesterday
Tomorrows can help yesterday's stain

Tears of laughter not sorrow sawn
Laughter from pleasure not cruelty borne
Treasure the child who looks up to you
Treasure the child you carried—born new
Yesterday is the past we never forget
Tomorrow make it a day without regret

Tomorrow is not a given day
But one we should never portray
For when wrong is done in yesterday
Tomorrows can help yesterday's stain

3 Gina, Me, and the Open Road

Again I was without a home and night had fallen. I walked aimlessly for a while, staying close to the garden fences and trying to avoid being seen. A figure approached and as we passed one another, I kept my head down to avoid eye contact until I heard a woman's voice speaking to me.

"Hello Sharon! It's been a long time! Are you going into town?"

I looked up, surprised to hear my name being spoken and looked into a familiar face from my school days. "Christ Gina! You scared the life out of me! What are you doing out so late?"

"Late?" Gina mocked, "Where the hell you been living? On the Moon? I am off into town—what about you? I see you have your bags with you; doing a runner?" she continued to mock.

"In town? A little late for that. I am off to my brother's, you remember Mark?"

We talked for a while. Gina was a year ahead of me in school and although we were never pals, we held a healthy respect for each other. Gina's father ruled her house with a rod of iron and she often arrived at school bruised and dazed.

"Fancy a coffee?"

"A little late for that isn't it? Nowhere open this time of night."

"Christ Shazza! Where you been living? It's only eleven thirty! The night's still young! Come on! I know were the late night diners are."

"I suppose it will be OK; all right, a quick cuppa."

As we entered the diner, I noticed the looks of others and the judgments made by our dress. I was a real plain Jane with straggly long dark hair listless from lack of washing. My clothes were creased and torn from lack of concern. In truth, I had no respect or pride in my appearance.

We chatted for what seemed like hours. Gina spoke about her family and the terrible beatings, but I kept quiet about my past, preferring to allow Gina to think I was fine. "I have to go Sharon, I need to earn some money or I won't be eating tomorrow. By the looks of you, eating is not a problem."

I was taken aback by Gina's forwardness about my increased weight. *Cheeky bastard*, I thought. "Where do you work Gina?" I noticed Gina thinking hard before she answered.

"I work the streets."

"Doing what?"

"Making sure my clients are satisfied so they come back for more. Come on Shazza, do I look dressed for a night on the town? Or even a housewife."

I think I got the gist of her renditions of employment as I scanned her attire. Her skirt short, very short—in fact one could quite well believe she wore only the belt. Her top cut low, very low, exposing ample breasts. Her shoes clip clopped on the pavement as her long lean legs took strides that had me jogging to keep up. But I did not want to make an assumption for fear of being wrong and getting bashed for my impure thoughts.

"Are you being sarcastic or are you really that stupid?" Gina teased, again making me blush with embarrassment.

"No, really! I don't know what you mean."

"I'm a bad girl," Gina laughed, "A prostitute, slut, and whore… whatever you want to label me."

Her answer shocked me and I was totally lost for words, "Oh, that's nice," I heard myself say. I could have kicked myself when those words flowed from my lips. *Oh shit! Oh that's nice! Jesus, Shaz! Get a grip—you sound like a dork*, I thought to myself as I tried smiling sweetly

"Wow Shazza! That's the first time I have ever had that reaction. I guess you're in shock. What's your job?"

"I'm a nanny." I was still trying to absorb Gina's profession. I had read about prostitutes and their pimps and they seemed hard people—not the sort you want to get involved with. Drugs, drinking, and killing people. They inhabited a seedy world run by the mafia.

"How did you end up getting into prostitution?" I inquired, genuinely interested.

"My uncle was taking it for nothing. When I was fifteen, I finally decided, 'Fuck you, I am going to make people pay for it!' Lots of money to be had Shazza, and lots of punters ready willing, and bloody able."

I was in awe of Gina and looked up to her with respect. She seemed afraid of nothing and nobody! How I wished I were more like her instead of resembling a frightened rabbit caught in the headlights of an oncoming car. Gina reminded me of a stag—strong, proud and fearful of nothing.

"What about your pimp? Does he beat you up?"

She shrieked with laughter.

"A pimp? You've been watching too much television, Shaz! Bloody hell, you really are funny! You make me laugh. I don't have a pimp." Gina laughed out loud again.

I was a little annoyed that Gina mocked my innocence so harshly, but was also slightly afraid because I was aware of how streetwise prostitutes were and of how hard Gina appeared to be.

"You have nowhere to sleep, have you Shaz?"

"How did you know?"

"I guess the bags gave it away. You can stay at my place if you wish."

"Who's there with you?"

"I live on my own. Do you want to, or not?"

I decided to take her up on the offer. Walking beside Gina made me feel safe but also ugly as the men ogled her every step, attention I was glad for her to receive. Over the next few days we shared many thoughts and inner secrets. Gina was amazed I was still a virgin at age seventeen.

"How can you still be a virgin if your old man sexually abused you?"

I explained.

"That's fucking perverse, Shaz! Even my punters would not force me to do that! Your mother needs to be shot—she should have protected you! Bloody hell, it's hard to believe all that was going on!" Her words made me cry.

"What's wrong? I didn't mean to make you cry! Christ, don't be so bloody sensitive."

"Don't you believe me?"

"Of course I do! No one as fucked in the head as you could have come from The Waltons' family." We both fell about laughing; *The Waltons* was a television program that revolved around a healthy, wholesome American family.

"Are you working tonight?"

"Yes. I wish I could change my job sometimes, but I don't know anything else—why don't you give it a go? You could earn some good money."

"Not bloody likely! No man is touching me, I would kill him first!" I declared vehemently, filling with rage at the mere thought or suggestion.

We shared our dreams and aspirations with each other. Gina had always wanted to leave Devon and envied me my adventure. I knew there was a big, wide world out there and I hankered for the open road too. I met some wonderful people when I lived with Gina. I was once scornful and judgmental of tramps and bag-ladies, believing they were dirty, inconceivably nasty criminals who stole and mugged good citizens. How wrong I was, I was shown compassion and respect from the very people I had wronged. Thinking back to my home life, I now realize I was safer with these strangers who lived in their cardboard city, than the family God gave me.

Mandy was a bag-lady who smelt strongly of body odor and remnants of the fire lit in her steel trashcan the night before to keep out the cold. She had a shopping-cart with various bags of her belongings in it; she would allow no one near it. Basil was a tramp who had a reputation of being aggressive and unpredictable toward people. I knew him as a gentleman who was kind and elegant as he twirled me around, dancing and singing to the music that echoed through the walls of the surrounding nightclubs.

I felt safe amongst these people society chose to chastise and ridicule because many came from backgrounds similar to mine. None of us chose to live on the streets, none of us chose to have the sky as our blanket, and a smelly doorway or alley for our sleeping quarters. I was lucky I had Gina's apartment to go back to when the cold night's air snapped her jaws around my ankles. Three months had passed and life seemed easier, but my eating habits changed yet again. Now I ate very sparsely. Gina seemed depressed and worried about something.

"Let's do it. Let's just pack up and go! What's stopping us? We can go to Peterborough. You had friends there. We can maybe stay with them until we decide to move on to somewhere else."

"You make it sound too easy, Gina. Are you sure? I don't want to give this up to become bloody homeless again."

In truth, I wanted to leave Devon. I had nothing to keep me here. My brother Mark was very much involved with Mother and his attitude toward me was damning to the extreme. I had stayed with him a few times, but his anger toward me was too hurtful. Mark's rejection was difficult to cope with. We fought hard and I would never walk away without verbally fighting back. We blamed each other for the past and dealt with it best we could. Even now, I don't understand why we fought so hard against each other, but sometimes the words he used were horrendous and cutting. The two people in my life I believed would always be there were Mark and Paul. How wrong and stupid I was!

Eventually, we packed our bags. It took every penny we had to buy a pair of one-way train tickets to Peterborough. I had a friend, Tracy, who had told me to call her anytime I was in the area. However, I failed to tell Gina that I had lost contact with her. As the train chugged into the station late that evening and we got ready to board, I secretly hoped I would find my father on my travels. Of course, I had no idea what he looked like or even if he would welcome me. We were both like children filled with wonderment as we boarded the train to begin our adventure—it was nice to be leaving with a companion for a change.

The early hours of the morning took their toll and we fell asleep exhausted. I slept very lightly, waking with each little noise heard over the steady, droning rhythm of the wheels on the track. The sound of other passengers walking up and down the corridor of the carriage kept me awake.

I studied Gina as she slept and realized she was a pretty girl and needed no makeup. Her long brown hair fell over her face as the train gently rounded the bend of the track. I wondered *what horrors has she lived through and how many of us were out there trying to resolve the demons bequeathed to us from others? What was my place in this vast universe what did God have in store for me, was there a God at all?* I wiped away the condensation on the window and saw my reflection staring back from the dark abyss. *Would I ever trust a man enough to marry him?* I tried visualizing my husband to-be out there somewhere.

The train arrived in Peterborough at six in the morning; the fresh easterly wind whipping our hair as we stepped onto the platform. The smell of the diesel rushed up my nostrils while the smoke from the funnels swirled above our heads. We decided to sit on the platform and share a bottle of Coke between us while we took stock of the day ahead.

"We'll go to Tracy's house at nine; it's a more appropriate hour to visit."

"Is it very far from the station Shaz, or are we able to walk?"

"We can walk," I assured her.

Upon arrival outside Tracy's home, I was filled with excitement. It was nice to know Gina needed me for guidance for a change; this area was unfamiliar to her. Knocking on the door, I grinned smugly to myself knowing that Tracy would be surprised! I held my breath.

The door opened and an unfamiliar face appeared from behind it.

I listened stupefied as we were informed that Tracy had moved three weeks previously and no forwarding address had been left. Closing the gate behind us, I sank to the ground in total disbelief! We had given up everything in Devon and now we had nowhere to go. Gina was furiously shouting and cursing—I thought she would have a heart attack, she was so angry.

"There must be someone else we can visit."

I had no one else. Tracy was my only friend and we had neither money nor home and didn't know what we were going to do now.

"Don't ask me! I don't bloody know!" Gina was angry.

I was a little apprehensive when she suggested we could hitchhike. "No, Gina. It's too dangerous; there has to be another way."

"Well you can stay there sitting on the sidewalk—I'm off to the nearest bus station. Where is it?" she demanded.

"Why the bus station?"

"Because they will be able to tell me where the nearest gas station is and we can hitch a lift on one of the overnight trucks, dummy. Don't you know anything? And don't be expecting me to get you home either!" Gina's voice was raised condescendingly.

I pointed toward the bus station and Gina began walking, striding with attitude and swinging her arms like a soldier on parade. I watched as my friend walked further away from me. When she was almost out of sight, she shouted over her shoulder, "Are you coming?" without a backwards glance. I jumped at the invitation and hurried to catch up, making sure I stayed a little behind; she had made it clear that she did not want to look at my face.

"Don't be showing me your ugly mug and keep your ass behind mine! Don't talk to me either!"

I was beginning to feel as I did when living at home, I knew Gina could be violent and maybe I had provoked this rage. We rounded the corner and the bus station came into view. A few parked trucks were loitering. Gina went over and spoke to the drivers and I hung back, trying to not overstep the mark.

"He's going to take us to Bristol, but he's not leaving until late this afternoon, he has to pick up a load. We will have to hang around for the day."

"I don't think we should. It's dangerous! We could be murdered or raped. We could end up in a pervert's car."

Gina slapped me hard across my face!

"For Christ's sake! Get a grip! Not everyone is like that! Don't be so bloody naïve." I wasn't sure what frightened me more, Gina or hitchhiking.

I was stunned into silence by Gina's actions and the coming events. I didn't speak for a few hours and believed that she was about to leave me. Eventually, we got a lift with another truck driver who was leaving earlier and headed toward London. The driver was friendly, although I did not speak with him. I simply listened to them talking and wished I were more confident and outgoing—like Gina.

The driver dropped us off in a busy area of London. The clubs and streets were lit up like Christmas and the atmosphere was compelling. Many people walked the streets, all rushing to somewhere. Gina advised me to look for road signs that directed us southwest. We walked for a while. I liked this city, it was full of energy. I had heard that the streets were paved with gold, but never did understand what that meant.

"Here's the right slip road for the southwest, it says South," I excitedly informed Gina glad I had become useful. We can start thumbing."

"Aren't you hungry Gina? I could eat a horse." We hadn't eaten for two days.

"I suppose. Bloody hell Shaz, Tracy wouldn't have recognized you anyways because you're so skinny now. When I think of how fat you were a few months ago, I'm sure of it."

Soon a car stopped and the driver asked where we were going. Gina arranged with the man to take us to the right slip road for the southwest; we were heading the wrong way. As promised, Gina sat in the front with the driver. He asked if we were interested in working for him.

"What sort of job?" I asked.

"Waiting on tables, serving drinks."

"I don't think I would be any good at that type of work," I answered. Besides, I was underage and couldn't work in a bar.

"Stop the fucking car!" Gina shouted.

I started to panic, "What's the matter?"

"Stop this car right now!" I watched Gina reach for something on the driver's seat. I was scared witless by the scene unfolding before me in the front seat, believing she had gone completely insane.

"Stop the car or they come off! Don't fuck with me!"

I started pounding the window with both fists, hopelessly trying to catch the attention of the driver in the car beside us. The car stopped. I tried to open the door, but nothing happened. I looked to Gina who still had her arm reaching out toward the driver. He was now cursing; he was going to kill both of us, slit our throats and feed us to the animals in the zoo.

I looked over the driver's shoulder and was horrified to see that Gina had his genitals held firmly, her knuckles white with the pressure applied. The driver was sweating and Gina looked like someone possessed, her eyes wide, staring at him as though she were boring into his very soul. No wonder this man wanted to cut our throats.

"Oh my God, Gina! Put him down! What's wrong with you?" I screamed.

"Shut up you stupid bitch! Open the door, asshole, or the nuts go."

The driver revved the engine and shot forward then slammed on the brakes, causing me to shoot forward too. My mouth started to bleed as I connected with his head. Gina still had his nuts in her hands and he screamed in agony. He was seething and spitting vile intentions toward both of us.

"Sharon, get out!" Gina yelled with urgency. Again I tried the car door but it still would not open. I was crying, my mind went blank as fear overtook any rational thinking.

"Help me!" I screamed while frantically banging on the car window.

"Open the doors! Now!" Gina snarled at the driver.

I suddenly felt the warmth trickle of urine beneath me as I unexpectedly lost control of my bladder; now I was really going to get a beating from the driver. I heard a clicking sound and the driver snarled, "Its open! Piss off the pair of you! Whores!"

I jumped out of the car and ran out to the center of the road, afraid to look back. I stood there in the middle of the road, clasping my bag and crying hysterically, trying to stop a passing motorist and wondering why Gina had attacked the driver. The car sped off. Gina was on the pavement. I was afraid to approach her—had she gone completely insane?

"You all right, Shaz? Fucking hell, you pissed yourself!"

I was embarrassed by her remark and became aware that people were looking at me. Traffic drove around me as I stood rooted to the road, afraid to move either way.

"Why did you do that Gina? What's wrong with you?" I shouted.

Gina explained the man was a pimp and was trying to get us to work for him. I never knew how she knew his intentions, but was thankful I was with her that night because I probably would have accepted his offer.

We sat on the pavement watching people pass by, the silence broken when I spoke. "The nuts go!" I imitated her. "Jesus, Gina!" We started to laugh hysterically and relaxed a little.

"You know what really makes me fucking angry with that jerk?"

"No, what makes you angry with him?"

"He got me to hold his balls for nothing; I normally charge a fiver."

At first I was shocked, but then we rolled about the pavement laughing uncontrollably again; people passing skirted a large circle around us.

We made our way back to the right road and had a long wait before us. We had been trying to catch a ride for two hours and the dawn was breaking. Gina had fallen asleep on the grass, but I was afraid to close my eyes. I managed to change out of my wet clothing in the shadows of the night and had thrown away my sodden underwear. My upper lip was swollen and a small chip was missing from my top front tooth but I was glad to be alive. I was starting to think maybe Gina did have the right idea.

Finally, a truck stopped and offered to take us as far as Bristol, so we climbed into the cabin, happy to get out of the cold. About an hour later the driver pulled off the motorway and turned onto a dirt track. I started to get suspicious and sensed something was about to happen. He parked the truck at the end of the dirt track by some dumpsters; I grabbed the newspaper from the dashboard. Gina stretched her arms into the air and allowed the driver to rub her tummy.

"You're a bit tubby round the waist," he teased.

"I am pregnant."

"Where's the father?"

I was shocked by eavesdropping on Gina's revelation and even more intrigued by her next one.

"I don't know who the father is."

I was aware of the driver's hands fumbling around, a movement I knew all too well. I opened the cab door and jumped out.

"What are you doing?" Gina questioned.

"He's masturbating!" I pointed an accusing finger at the driver.

"No, I am not," he lied as he hastily put his clothing right. "Get out you little prick-teasers!" He pushed Gina toward the door and she jumped out of the cab. He quickly reversed the truck, knocking a few garbage cans over in his haste.

Gina was angry with me for losing our lift and punched me hard in the face, yelling that she could have handled it. I thought I was going to pass out with the pain as her punch reopened the cut from the previous evening.

"My bags! The bastard's got my bags! You fucking idiot, Sharon!"

I said nothing, afraid to provoke the situation any further and stunned that Gina punched me. I didn't dare broach the subject of her pregnancy either. We walked back to the motorway and found Gina's bag thrown in the ditch and without conversation, walked to thumb another lift.

Eventually, we got another ride. This driver was very nice and totally different from the last two; he gave us some fruit to eat and dropped us in the center of our own town. For once, I was glad to be on familiar soil. Gina booked us into a bed and breakfast, saying, "Tomorrow we can go and make a claim for money from the government. They will also pay for the room."

Gina was going out for a while. She explained that she needed to see some people—Union Street was her destination.

"I don't know what I would have done without you Gina; I have no idea how to go about doing any of these things."

"You will learn. Why don't you come with me? I need to go and see some people, get some money."

"I don't think so. I have never been inside a pub I mean."

"Shaz, stop winding me up! Of course you have been to a pub, everyone has."

"Not me. I have waited outside of one for Taff, but I've never gone inside one to drink, honest! Besides, I am underage."

Gina started to laugh and talked me into going with her. She was right; I needed to start going out more. We made our way down to the center of town. I felt a little paranoid about walking down this street. I had never been to this part of town but I had heard many stories and was warned by my parents to never come here. "If they could see me now, my mom would have had a frigging fit."

"Well you can please yourself! It's nothing to do with anyone, what you do."

Gina was right. It had nothing to do with anyone! I faltered only slightly as we entered the pub. I immediately disliked the reek of stale beer and cigarettes. Sawdust covered the floor and a large lady sat on a stool in a corner. She beckoned Gina over.

"Wait here, Shaz. I won't be a minute." She left me standing at the bar, giving me no time to object. This was not as glamorous as I had hoped, all the men looked old and slimy. I saw that the ceiling and walls were stained yellow from nicotine. I looked over toward Gina, but she had disappeared. As I scanned the room for some sign of her, an old man approached me. "So, you're the new one?"

"New? New... what?" I asked, my voice barely a whisper, but knew what he meant. My heart was pounding fast; I thought it would jump out of my chest. I did not want to believe Gina could do this to me. "I want to go," I whispered.

"What? Speak up, new–*un*," the ugly old man mocked.

I tried to walk away but my legs would not budge.

"What's wrong with you, too stuck up to have a drink with me?" The man was getting agitated, but I had already decided to fight this idiot; I was not going to have a drink with him!

I managed to walk to the door but as I tried to open it, another man put his arm against it to stop me from leaving.

"I will phone the police if you don't let me out!" I was crying and people in the pub burst into laughter.

"I will phone the police. Oh, will you now?" someone mimicked.

"Don't come in my pub threatening us, sweetheart."

Someone from behind the bar shouted to let me go and declared that I was not worth it. The man opened the door and slowly I walked into the safety of the street, breathing the fresh night air and glad to be in the open once more. I hated this town and the people in it. I waited for Gina in the entrance of the flats across the road, hiding in the shadows from prying eyes. Gina eventually turned up an hour later across the street and when she saw me, she started ranting about my performance in the pub earlier.

I walked up to her and punched and kicked her until she lay on the ground cowering. Eventually, someone dragged me off her and she was taken to the local hospital.

Later, when I visited her in the hospital, I lost control and started yelling at her. "I can't believe all you have done to me! All the times you've hit me and shouted at me, belittled me even. I took it all because I was afraid of you! I have put up with so much because I was afraid of people! Well not anymore!"

"Please keep your voices down," the nurse ordered.

"Shaz, I am sorry!" Gina was crying but I felt nothing, I didn't care.

"I trusted you and you set me up! I never want to see you again!"

"Please wait! Let me explain!" She sounded genuinely upset. "I had no choice; it didn't start that way!" She went on to explain that the fat lady was the madam of the street and Gina had owed her money. If I agreed to work for her, the debt would be wiped out.

"You bitch! We all have a choice, Gina!"

"Please Sharon, can we try again? I promise never to do that again! I don't want to lose your friendship!"

I needed to be alone. I was going outside for a cigarette. We could continue this discussion but now I needed a break from it.

I sat alone on a small wall outside the casualty unit, weighing my options. I could go back to being alone and frightened or stay with her and try again. I lit my cigarette and puffed on it thoughtfully. When I went back into the hospital, I knew what was best for me.

"Ok. One last chance. If you promise never to do that to me again, I will respect the way you choose to live, providing you do the same." We reached an understanding.

Gina still tried to put me down at times, but the truth was, we needed each other more than each were prepared to admit, but I was about to meet someone who would change my life forever.

The Basics of Life

Tears of sorrow, tears of pain
for memories that linger from yesterday

We cry for our own sorrow and pain,
not for the ones who no longer remain

We grow and carry children of our own
and promise to look after—no matter what they oppose

Days to weeks will pass untold.
when words are spoken that others bestow
Days to weeks and weeks to months,
till we don't remember what caused the crunch

Anger, pain, frustrations, will fade
and in their place bitterness gains
We start to forget why we know longer talk
The months turn to years and our loved ones no-more.
It's not until we get the call
and find our cherished ones have left this world
We cry our tears for what has been lost,
"if only" rings round our thoughts at a cost

We don't remember, we don't want to be told
We stand where we are because we welcomed the cold!

We need to think and swallow our pride,
does the end justify this human tide?
Its waters crashed onto land
and everything became way out of hand
I could have said, "I disagree,"
and walked away calmly letting anger settle in thee

Or maybe waited until the others were torn,
from the anger they saw when the words were fawned.

Life's too short we need all the friends we can get
Don't stand at their graveside with only regrets!

4   Not Yet a Woman

I ventured away from home only when it was time for work; I was employed as a trainee chef and was enjoying it immensely. Things finally started to look up for me and my life was beginning to take some direction. Gina was still earning her money on the streets and sometimes would not return home for days. Although this was not an ideal way to live, I was still happier than I had ever been.

We were permanent residences at the 'Guesthouse' and Gina had made friends with the pump attendant who worked in the nearby garage. Their friendship was platonic and often they allowed me to tag along. I felt quite at ease with Ian and over the weeks, I spoke more to him, sometimes even visiting him without Gina.

One evening I noticed Gina waiting at the main door of the guesthouse when I returned home from work. "What are you doing? What's the matter?"

"We've been kicked out; they found out I was bringing punters back."

"They can't throw me out too! I've done nothing wrong!" I protested. "I need this place! It's all I have! How will I get ready for work?"

"Let it go, Shaz. We can just book into another guesthouse."

"No, I won't! I am fed up with people pushing me around! I am going to talk to them!" I rang the doorbell and the owner appeared.

"Why have you thrown me out? I have done nothing wrong! You have no right to do this!" I could feel my pulse racing and the adrenalin rushing.

"I have every right! I don't run a brothel and I won't have your sort living under my roof!"

I was ready to explode, "My sort?" I retaliated, "What the bloody hell do you mean *my sort?* You jumped-up asshole!"

"If the cap fits! Get rid of your friend, the more you hang around with her, the more the mud will stick," the owner screamed back rancorously, slamming the door forcefully in my face.

It had not occurred to me that people would assume I was a prostitute. Gina started swearing and kicking the door.

"Come outside, you old fart! You're no better than me!" I wanted to get hold of this idiot who judged me so wrongfully and slam the truth home in his face. Rage coursed through me and I started to lose control of myself as my demons took over my emotions. Gina pulled me out of the front garden and tried to calm me down but I was too angry to listen! Life was unfair! I was fed up with the continuous fight just to survive! Every time I thought things were getting better, something happens to hold me down in that dark place I had lived for nearly seven years. I was beginning to have thoughts about ending it all, images of a better life in another dimension looked more and more appealing.

We walked around for a while desperately trying to think of a solution.

"I'm going to the pub for a drink; are you coming?"

"No, I think I'll go and see Ian—he may know of a guesthouse for tonight. We'll meet up with you later, about ten." I made my way slowly toward the petrol station, depression consuming me. How was I ever going to stop this cycle? I desperately wanted my own home, a place to call my own. I considered asking Mark for help, but did I really want to go there again?

I stopped to rest, perching myself on a wall and lit a cigarette. My life had no constructive future and I was afraid of eventually finding myself working beside Gina, but being a virgin and fearing the loss of it, kept me from taking that step. Gina always had money, never did drugs and was spotlessly clean. A total contrast to what I had believed working girls were like.

I thought about Stepfather and all he had taken from me. He not only took my childhood innocence, but my family and my future. He destroyed Sharon Arscott many years ago. His life had continued happily as before, yet so much pain always surged through my body. I believed my heart would shatter. I then thought of mother and wondered what it would be like to have her arms around me. She must love me a little; after all, I am her daughter. I still wanted her love so desperately that I was physically unable to function at times.

I continued on my way to the garage, feeling totally beaten by life. Ian greeted me as I entered the kiosk.

"Hi Sharon! What're the bags for?"

I burst into tears and spilled the ugly events that had taken place.

"Sometimes Ian, I think it would be easier to just do what Gina does, at least I would have money and a roof over my head."

"Yeah, maybe you're right, but you aren't the type. Now dry your tears. I will open one of the show cars for you so you won't have to worry where you'll sleep tonight." He explained I would have to be gone by seven in the morning because the day shift would start arriving soon after. When Gina arrived at eleven, I told her about Ian's proposal.

"It's about time you started looking after yourself, Shaz. Do you realize you are sitting on a bloody gold mine?" she asked cryptically.

I didn't understand and Ian tried to explain; I was embarrassed and very angry once I got the gist of it.

I had a fretful sleep that night. Ian kept our bags in his car so we would not have to lug them around during the day. I went to work but found it increasingly hard to concentrate so I made an excuse to leave two hours early. As I walked along the beach, I tried to think of some sort of solution and I was slipping into depression while my thoughts were continuously pulled back into my past. How was I ever going to trust anyone or enjoy a normal relationship? I didn't like being this way—I hated the way I was! I considered every man to be a potential rapist and any act of kindness had a hidden agenda.

Looking out toward the horizon, I smiled to myself; the last time I was here, I believed in my heart that it would be the last. Some things never change and as always, the sea gave me that little bit of hope, its hidden power and strength inspiring me.

"Hi Sharon! How's your day been? You look tired, have you been crying?" I had wandered back to the garage and Ian's friendly face greeted me.

"Hello Ian." I shook my head as Gina came in. "Hi everyone," Gina interrupted, "How was work, Sharon?" The atmosphere between us was tense. Gina announced that she had found somewhere to stay for a few days; I was welcome to go with her.

"Where? How long have you known them"?

"Get down off your high horse Sharon and don't look a gift horse in the mouth! He's a friend. His name is Peter and he lives with another bloke, take it or leave it."

"Shush, don't say anything! Here comes the mechanic on call for the night," indicating with a glance toward a young man entering the garage. "Don't mention anything about sleeping in the cars!" Ian panicked.

The man came to the reception area and asked if there were any calls for him then turned to me and started to flirt. "Would you like a ride in my breakdown truck?"

"You don't have a chance with that cold fish" Gina butted in sarcastically, "she's the original virgin—but I wouldn't mind."

The man ignored her and continued to talk with me. I found his manner quite pretentious. He and Gina wound up going for the drive and I watched as they drove off. He must think I'm a real idiot. *How she could embarrass me like that?* I wondered. Ian asked if I would ever consider going for a drive with the man.

"No, I don't think so. He's a little weird." He looked like a hippy and seemed very forward in his manner.

Ian said his name was Mike and that he lived with his parents and that was all he knew.

"Where is your family, Sharon? You never speak of them, and I can tell you don't belong with Gina; you two have nothing in common."

"We have more in common than you think. She's helped me through some pretty hard times when no one else cared. Underneath, she's a pretty good person but she just doesn't show it."

Ian said he would let us sleep in the car after Mike returned with Gina and had gone home. However, Mike didn't leave as expected. To our surprise, he stayed all night and left only when the dawn was breaking. As he drove off the forecourt, I was unsure what my thoughts about him were. We had talked for hours and my first impression of him had changed. Gina and I made our way to Peter's house; which turned out to be located only a few streets away from mother's street. Gina produced a key and said Peter had given it to her yesterday when I asked.

The bedroom we shared was small but I felt at ease here. Gina had explained that Peter and Andrew were a couple. I decided that I needed to speak frankly to Gina as we sat in our room. I explained I did not want to leave this home too. "You can't bring anyone back to this room and nobody is to touch my bed." We agreed to respect each other's space.

"I don't want you thinking I am going to sort everything out either, Shaz." She explained that we could only stay for two months and had to pay seven pounds weekly toward rent and food and, "I don't want you moaning at me if you're left alone. Not all men are bastards, and while we are on the subject of men!" her voice was rising, "I stepped in with Mike because I did not think you could handle him. You are such the prissy one; next time I won't bother."

I knew we were approaching the parting of ways; it was just a matter of time. Gina threw my bag onto my bed and said she would be back later. I ran a bath, phoned work to let them know that I would be back tomorrow, and then went to relax in the tub. After the hot bath, I retired to my room. It was noon and I was exhausted. I realized that I had not met the owner of the house yet, but was too tired to care. I slipped between the crisp, clean sheets and fell into a deep sleep until seven the following morning.

I was confused for an instant when I awoke. Gina's bed was empty. I dressed and made my way downstairs, straining to hear what the deep voices were saying. I was nervous about facing the men of the house. *How I wish Gina were here!* I realized how much I depended on her. Cautiously, I opened the lounge door and looked in on a clean but sparsely furnished room. The door to the kitchen stood open. The back door suddenly slammed shut and the voices fell quiet, but I could hear that someone was still puttering around in the kitchen.

"Maybe it's Gina. Here goes," I whispered to myself.

"Hello. You must be Sharon, I'm Pete. I see that Gina is not with you."

I nodded and grunted, too shy to speak and now certain this man was not gay. I queried him about Andrew, but Peter did not seem to get what I was trying to ask.

"I'll see you tonight. I am off to work now; the spare key is hanging for you—I don't know how big G is going to get in."

"Big G?" I asked.

"Gina! We call her Big G, duh! You're slow!" He pointed to his chest; I laughed nervously trying not to sound shocked. I busied myself in the kitchen and hearing the front door closing behind him was a relief. I ran up the stairs to check the other two bedrooms.

"The lying bitch!" I shouted. Both men had separate bedrooms and on the bedside table was a picture of Peter with a woman—and she certainly was not his mother. She was beautiful and was looking admiringly into Peter's eyes. Peter was slim and tall with a mope of brown hair and a small mustache. I gathered my workbag and dashed to the bus stop, seething inside.

After work, I made my way back home. Gina should be there; wait until I speak to her! I was still angry. When I opened the front door, I smelled food cooking and was greeted by a woman sitting in one of the armchairs in the lounge. She was quite large, although her greasy hair was the first thing I noticed. Her dress sense showed a lot to be desired and her shoes were scuffed on the toes.

"Hello, you must be Gina? Or Sharon?" the lady queried.

"It's Sharon. Nice to meet you. You are...?" I left the question hanging.

"Mary, I am Andrew's girlfriend and just to let you know he is not available."

"Available? Available for *what?*" I answered sarcastically. The atmosphere felt frosty and I sensed Mary's animosity toward me. Andrew appeared from the kitchen and introduced himself. I was laughing inside at Mary's comment about Andrew's availability. He was about six feet tall with black shoulder length hair and his trousers had at least a month's food wiped down each front panel. His shirt gone grey with lack of care. After a few minutes, everyone began to finally relax. These people were a lot older than me, they had to be at least late twenties, ancient, and I felt a little uneasy in their company.

"So Sharon, do you work the same job as Gina?"

"I am training as a chef. Why, do you work with Gina?" I replied defensively. How dare this idiot try to belittle me in front of Andrew! Mary explained how Peter had met Gina; he was one of her punters. I was uneasy with the conversation. I wished Mary and I were alone having this discussion. Talking so openly about Gina's job in mixed company was embarrassing me; I also did not like the way Mary was judging Gina.

I left the house informing Andrew I would return later that night—I could come and go as I pleased. Making my way to the garage to see Ian, I felt miserable—it seemed that so many people were eager to judge and condemn. I was glad to see his smiling face he always smelled fresh and looked immaculately clothed. We talked for a while, stopping only when a customer came in; the headlights of another car lit up the Kiosk.

"Oh, it's just Mike again. He's on breakdown detail tonight so he won't stay long." Ian was worried that Mike would report him for having people in the kiosk; it was strictly against company rules.

"Hello again! Haven't seen you around for a few days." He spoke very softly; I felt instantly shy and bowed my head to avoid eye contact.

"Have you seen Gina?" I asked nervously, trying to strike a conversation.

"Who's Gina?"

"She was the girl you took for a ride in the truck, Mike!" Ian laughed.

"Oh my God, no! I wanted to take this lady but the other one jumped in!" Turning to me, he now asked if I would like to go to the pictures with him one night.

"No, I can't. I have to work," I lied. Mike started to tease. Ian sensed my shyness and suggested we all go together but we would have to wait to ask Gina. Mike left the garage and I watched until he drove out of view.

"You like him, don't you?" I was embarrassed by Ian's suggestion. Mike was six feet tall, his hair dark as ebony and wild—a bit of a hippy and very lean. His brown bell bottom trousers and tank-top looked quite neat. His shirt had the widest collar and cuffs I had ever seen.

"What's your ideal man, Sharon?"

I thought for the longest time but could not answer the question; I had nothing to compare my ideal man to.

"Hello you two!" We were interrupted by a familiar voice.

"Gina, where have you been?" She had met a client who took her away for a few days. We discussed our plans to go to the pictures together and agreed that all four of us would go Saturday night. Ian agreed to inform Mike the following morning.

Gina then explained why she lied about Peter and Andrew. "So you see Sharon, you would have been homeless. Sometimes we have to take chances—besides, you're not their type at all" I knew Gina was right—had I known they were heterosexual; I would never have gone there.

Saturday arrived and Gina and I were looking forward to going out together, something we rarely did. I made a special effort.

"Christ Sharon! You look really nice tonight! You should wear makeup more often!"

"Do you think it's over the top? I don't want Mike to get the wrong impression." I was secretly excited; this was my first night out on a date. Gina had given her word to not leave me alone with him.

We took our seats in the picture house; Gina and I sat beside each other, Mike sat next to me followed by Ian on the other side of Mike. I was a little uneasy with the seating arrangements.

No one spoke as the lights dimmed and Mike slowly moved his arm behind me, making me feel uneasy. Very slowly, I moved forward. He then moved his hand onto my knee. Sheer terror raced through me as he softly tried to caress my leg. I crossed my leg and made his hand fall. This confused him. What was my problem? He was getting a little agitated by my behavior.

Again, he tried to place his hand on my arm and I froze as he slowly stroked my arm and searching for my hand to hold. I started to whimper.

"Please don't do that," but he ignored me and continued to move his hand over my arm.

"Don't!" I yelled.

"Oh stop being a foolish child," he teased. I got up and quickly made my way to the toilets, followed by Gina.

"I saw what happened and you have to learn to lighten up Sharon. He was just trying to hold your hand. You are going to end up old and lonely if you don't get your act together."

"I can't help it! I don't know how to react! I keep thinking he is using me for one thing only; it frightens me! I don't like being this afraid!"

Gina went into the small cubicle and locked the door behind her. I turned to the mirror and studied my reflection; I looked hideous! How could anyone be attracted to me? Who was I trying to kid? He was after one thing only and I was not going to be used in that way! Gina called out, asking if I were still in the room, all had gone too quiet.

"I'm still here. What am I going to do? I can't face going back out there! He will think I am weird."

"Do you like him?" Gina inquired.

"Yes, I think so."

"Tell him why you are the way you are. If he has any respect for you, he will understand! Hell! You're nearly eighteen years old, don't allow the night devil to take any more from you!" She made it sound so easy; but I knew she was right.

"He may think I was to blame! He might think I was a dirty little slag who deserved it."

"I believe you; no one as messed up in their head as you are could have come from a good clean wholesome background. Gina had such a way with words and she lifted my spirits just by telling me that she believed me in such a definitive way as to leave no room for doubting her sincerity.

"Can I ask you something Gina? Something very personal?"

"Ok, but I don't always give straight answers," she joked, opening the door and making her way to the sink area to wash her hands.

"What happened to the baby you told the lorry driver you were expecting?"

"Oh that," she laughed out loud. "He said I was fat so I just gave an acceptable reason for it."

"I wish I had your gutsy attitude, and then I could do anything."

"Survival of the fittest Sharon; that's what life's all about! Use them before they use you. They get what they want then toss you aside—that's why I make them pay, only touch what you can afford, that's my motto."

"But surely, not all men are like that. Some must be OK?"

"Show me a man who cares, I mean *really cares*, but until then, I will 'use before being used'."

Gina had a point as far as I was concerned, but there was also sadness in the way she spoke. The door to the toilets opened and another woman walked in. "Come on; let's go back before they think we ditched them."

We huddled together in our seats, quietly chatting away about the wrongs and rights of the world and when the film finished, I decided to go straight home. Gina was going to work; as was Ian. I could wait on my own for the bus, or accept a lift from Mike.

I decided on the latter. A stony silence fell in the car all the way home, only broken when I gave Mike directions.

"This will be fine. I can walk the rest of the way." I did not want him to know where I lived. He asked if we could meet again and when I faced him, I saw that the streetlight was caught in his eyes. My heart started to race as his eyes seem to light up like crystals and I wanted to kiss him but was worried he would reject me because of my earlier performance. Instead, I angrily declared that he had no right to touch me like he had in the picture house and that if he were hoping for anything else, then he better start walking now; I was not that kind of girl.

"Where the hell is all this coming from? I'm not walking anywhere because this is *my* car and you can't blame me for wanting to hold your hand! Christ!" He protested his innocence. "How about we start again? I will come and pick you up tomorrow when I finish work, no strings attached—we will just have a drink and talk."

I agreed and then walked the rest of the way home. I felt a little proud of myself for letting Mike know how I felt, despite that it tumbled out all wrong because what I said was actually opposite of what I felt—I was in turmoil.

The following day passed slowly because I was excited about seeing him again. I checked my watch and saw that I had another three hours to wait.

"Gina, does my bum look fat in this? My stomach sticks out too much! How do my legs look in this?" and so it went, my insecurity rising and showing itself!

"For goodness sake, Sharon! You look good in everything! Let me sleep! I had a late night last night!" she shouted after me and threw her pillow at the door as I left the room.

"Ten more minutes and I'll be leaving; are you sure I look OK"?

"Yes! For the last time, just go! You look fine!"

I closed the front door and waited outside for Mike to arrive—and worried. I worried about getting into a car with someone I hardly knew. I worried that he would not show up at all. I felt like a child! I was also worried about bumping into Stepfather. So far, I had managed to stay clear of both mother and him by only going out after dark. I was thirty minutes early tonight so stayed hidden behind the array of bushes. I heard the sound of a car engine getting closer and my stomach started churning, my heart beating wildly. I acted casual as I settled into the front seat.

"Hope I didn't keep you waiting long," Mike smiled as he offered me a pretty bouquet.

"No, I just got here. Actually, I nearly forgot until Gina reminded me," I lied. I could smell his aftershave and knew it was Brut, the same aftershave my brother Mark wore. A stony silence once again fell between us as Mike drove toward the local Mooreland. I really did want to talk with him but I had lost my voice. I strained to peek at him sideways, hoping he would not notice. I noticed his mustache for the first time; his eyebrows were bushy his hair wild and shoulder length. His build was very wiry and he was six feet tall. He actually looked older than I first thought. He tried to make polite conversation; he said he lived with his parents. He also said he smoked marijuana. I had never met anyone who took illegal drugs before and was amazed that he looked normal. I had expected drug-users to sweat and curl up in the fetal position in a corner. Mike laughed at the images I described.

The more we dated, the more I liked him. I considered telling him about my past as, Gina suggested, but was afraid he would reject me. I knew the fluttering feelings I felt when he was around was love but Gina advised me to slow down; she said he was my first boyfriend and there would be many more after him. Mike was patient with me and more mature sexually, but he respected me. Besides, I was the first girl he had met that would not sleep with him, no matter how hard he tried. I felt I owed him an explanation of why I was reluctant to take the relationship any further and the opportunity presented itself one evening on a dinner date where there would be no interruptions. As we made our way toward the table, I worried about what would happen after I dropped the bombshell I had been secretly carrying and hiding from him and everyone.

"Mike, there's something I need to tell you. After I've told you, I'll understand if you don't want to see me anymore."

"You're starting to worry me, Sharon." He reached his hand across the table and briefly held mine, but I gently pulled my hand away. It would make it much more difficult for me to continue if he were holding my hand.

"Please be honest with me Mike—that's all I ask."

"Oh bloody hell! You are scaring me Sharon! For God's sake, just tell me!" He looked so worried and I hated being the cause! I hurried to continue.

I bowed my head because I couldn't bear to look at him as I explained why I had no family and told him what had happened to me in my house full of whispers. I was afraid to tell Mike because no one had ever believed me. Everyone I loved turned on me once I told them what my stepfather had done to me, and they each made me out to be nothing more than lying filth. Now I was opening myself up to losing Mike with the truth too. I was terrified because I had fallen in love with Mike and wanted his love in return. Now, I thought *he may be about to walk out of my life!*

But he didn't. Instead, Mike was shocked by my family's mistreatment toward me. He had come from a stable background with no abuse and it was hard for him to understand how parents could hurt their children this way. He admitted that he had thought something about me was not right. "Sometimes I saw a certain look in your eyes, sadness," he said.

He trusted me enough to know that what I told him was the truth and he passed the first test of many; I needed to know I could trust this man.

"You're with me now. He won't ever hurt you again." Mike said. He came over to put his arm around me. It felt good to have a comforting arm around me; I had been alone and uncomforted for too long.

Later, I was sad to watch Mike drive away after he dropped me off at home. *I should take Mike to meet my brother*, I considered. I was sure they would like each other. I was feeling more relaxed.

"How would you like to meet my parents?" Mike had taken the initiative first.

"It's about time. I was beginning to think you had made them up," I teased. Although I had known Mike for only ten weeks, I felt completely at ease in his company. Meeting his parents was a big thing for me—I wanted to make the right impression and took three hours to get ready. I tried on everything Gina and I owned. By the end, the bedroom looked like it had been ransacked!

"Bloody hell, Sharon, not again! It's only his parents! Slow down!" Gina begged, exasperated with me.

"Nothing fits me!" Since meeting Mike, I had lost so much weight—my eating disorder had spiraled out of control.

"You have gotten way too thin! Sharon, you need to start eating properly."

"I do eat! I just don't want to get fatter or Mike won't like me. Look how wobbly my legs are and how big my stomach is; it sticks out too far!" I complained as I examined my body in front of the mirror. I was ugly and fat and could not understand why Mike even wanted to be seen with me. I pushed the mirror away, disgusted by my revolting reflection.

A car horn sounded outside and I rushed to the window; it was Mike. I ran down the stairs with my heart pounding its own wild bongo beat! I wanted to pinch myself—this had to be a dream! Mike looked at me approvingly when I jumped into the car next to him. "You look nice," he complimented. "We're only going to meet my parents so don't expect anything special."

"It's only an old skirt and blouse I threw on. I was running a little late," I lied.

He parked outside his parents' home and I was surprised to learn they lived not far from me. In fact, I had visited friends who lived on this same street.

"Wait a minute. What are they like? What are they expecting me to be like?" I was getting nervous.

"They don't know you are coming. Do you want to leave it and come back another day?"

"No, come on then; let's go." I took a deep breath and forced myself to open the car door. I stood up, straightened my skirt and we walked, hand in hand, toward the front door. I felt physically sick; my stomach was in nervous knots. *What if they didn't like me? What if I did or said something wrong? What if...* What if's were causing chaos in my mind!

Mike opened the door and we stepped inside. Too late to turn back now! He introduced me to Jim and Yvonne, his parents. I liked them instantly.

Jim was a fine figure of a man and a dashing one at that. Evie was a sweet, petite lady full of grace and very polite in manner. Their pleasant personalities made it easy for me to feel instantly at ease with them. When left alone for a few minutes in the front room with Mike's father, I felt no fear or discomfort in his presence. They invited me to stay for dinner but I declined, too shy to eat in front of them. They politely invited me to visit again and I felt the invitation was sincere.

Days rolled by in a contented haze. After another evening together, Mike was beginning to show signs of frustration. I knew what the problem was and although we kissed and fooled around, he could easily and innocently say or do something that invoked terror in me. Each time I broke away and turned cold toward him, he felt hurt by my rejection. Mike was getting frustrated and even threatened to go elsewhere.

In self-defense and defiance, I told him to bugger off and do just that! He constantly told me that he loved me and I never doubted his feelings. I desperately wanted to tell him that I loved him too, but the words simply would not come. I also understood that although Mike properly showed revulsion toward my parents, he never really understood what abuse was, the enormity and complexity, the pain.

I unjustly felt used by Mike. When he tried to get closer, I felt sick to my stomach at the mere thought of him deriving pleasure from my body. I hated myself for the spiteful things that blurted from my mouth at times, but I had promised myself many years ago to sleep only with one man—my husband. This had nothing to do with being abused, but a personal choice for myself. Promiscuity was for other girls, not me. My feelings and actions were a constant source of frustration and confusion for myself as well—I was a contradiction on legs.

One night Mike was babysitting for Jane, his sister, and asked if I would join him. "We've known each other six months," he started.

"And your point is?" I snapped. If I thought Mike had engineered this time alone to gratify another round of frustration, I was leaving.

"It's just an observation." He abandoned whatever he was trying to say.

We settled down for the evening and talked about our dreams and aspirations. He handed me a brown paper bag and I excitedly tore it open as though Christmas had arrived. I held up a beautiful blue dress with a polka dot and flower print, the buttons were big and shinny and the lapels fell with grace; the latest fashion from C & A. I was speechless! Then suddenly, I was overwhelmed with emotion as a reality occurred to me unbidden. I burst into tears.

"What's wrong? Don't you like it? We can take it back. Did I pick the wrong size?" He struggled to understand.

I was too upset to talk as I sobbed uncontrollably and ran to the bathroom. I was so overwhelmed—how could I tell Mike?

My mind sunk back to the years when I would watch my sister open her gifts at Christmas and birthdays. My heart ached as I tried to catch my breath—I was going to have to tell Mike that, with the exception of the little gift exchange at Christmas while I was working as a nanny, his was the first present anyone has given me since the age of thirteen.

That night, I fell hopelessly in love with Mike and promised myself that no matter what happened, I would always keep the dress. Mike tapped on the bathroom door and asked if I were Ok. I emerged with the dress on, twirled and asked his opinion. He convinced me that I looked fine and placed his green leather hat on my head. "You look lovely! Can I take a photo?" I agreed even though I hated my picture being taken. I hated being reminded of the ugliness others saw when they looked at me.

Jane phoned to tell Mike that the car had broken down and that they would be very late and suggested we make a bed on the lounge floor and sleep the night. I had never been so nervous! Could I do this? The beds were made and it was made clear to Mike that I would sleep on the sofa and he would be on the floor. We turned the light off and settled down to sleep. I lay listening to his breathing and desperately wanted to join him on the floor.

"You comfortable?"

"Yep." I quickly snapped back! *Why the hell don't I just go and snuggle up beside him?* But the thought of approaching him made me feel cheap—I wished he would make another effort.

I sighed heavily and fidgeted, hoping Mike would make a suggestion. I tried to bore my feelings into his brain with a psychic link. He finally spoke!

"Are you sure you don't want to come and lay here beside me? I won't touch you."

"Ok, then." I tried to sound like I was giving in to his relentless insistence rather than the one simple invitation it really was. I gingerly made my way in the dark, afraid of accidentally touching his body and giving the wrong impression. He snuggled up behind me and I felt his naked flesh against me. I was a little surprised, but still relaxed and happy not to be frightened by the situation. Lying with Mike felt comfortable and natural and my heart fluttered with love for him.

He very gently turned me to face him and I could not resist. The time felt right for me because I loved him so much but it wasn't as romantic as I imagined it would be—it hurt like hell! I had read the first time described as earth moving or a tide rolling through you but I felt more like I was in the middle of a tsunami and I desperately tried to escape and break the union. Mike seemed to be hanging on for dear life.

Afterward, I ran to the downstairs bathroom, mortified. I didn't want to look at him and, wrapping myself in a towel, I tried to make a plan for my return. I needed to get my clothing but I was apprehensive about facing him. *Will he lose respect for me? Is this the last time I will see him now that he got what he wanted?* I felt no different than I did a few minutes ago and wondered what all the fuss was about. I sat on the edge of the bathtub while my mind swirled. I vacillated between elation about finally losing my virginity to deflation about losing my fantasy about saving myself for my husband. And the earth certainly had not moved, nor did I see fireworks. I checked in the mirror and was relieved that I didn't look different. I had always believed people would be able to look at me and know when I was no longer a virgin. Mike called to me, breaking this train of thought.

"I'm bleeding! I've cut myself," I lied.

I buried my head in a towel and rocked—even I knew most girls bled the first time. I called for him to turn off the light and I fumbled back in the dark, slipping next to him under the blanket.

His arms engulfed me and pulled me closer to him, "Are you all right?"

"I'm fine."

"I didn't hurt you, did I?" His voice was filled with concern.

"No." I assured him as I snuggled closer.

I considered this moment to be the start of my adult life. Only two years ago, I had no one, I was eighteen years old and dreading the future. I will add that after the lights went out for the second time, the earth did eventually move and fireworks were seen, but that's for my eyes only!

Passage of Time

Even the deepest of wounds can be healed with the passage
of time

Words are cutting, but also soothe
Actions destroying, but can set you free
The wounded heart fragile, the world we live in sometimes
cold
One moment of anger can last a lifetime of pain
It's the bitterness that lasts and not the memory of our foe
We have to let go of our pain and bury it within the grains of
sands
Watch the sea take your desolation as she snatches the grains
Deep within her belly hidden and buried forever
Her strength inequitable to any who dare to fight back

Even the deepest of wounds can be healed with the passage
of time!

5   Not My Baby

It had been seven weeks since we babysat for Jane. Our relationship was stormy at times and my emotional moods vacillated between highs and lows. I was a wreck and tried to hide it from Mike. Sometimes my words were hateful, but he was patient beyond human expectation. I wanted to cut out my tongue when venomous words seeped like acid from my mouth.

I was getting tired more easily and sometimes felt sick to my stomach. Gina suggested I might be pregnant, but I was sure she was wrong. Other than the first night, we had taken precautions. She insisted we go to the chemist and buy a new pregnancy kit that had just come on the market. We had to wait until the following morning for the results. Also, I would need to be at least six weeks overdue for a menstrual cycle for the results to be accurate. I explained to Gina that I had not had a menstrual cycle since I was about fourteen so I was fairly certain the results would be negative. Still, I was unable to sleep that night with mother's prediction reverberating around in my head.

"By the time you are twenty, you will have five babies, all with different fathers, and you will still be on your own."

I did not want a baby out of wedlock! This was turning out all wrong! I jumped out of bed at six a.m., unable to endure the anticipation of not knowing any longer! I was not ready for the responsibility of a child. It was at times like these when I yearned for a mother of my own—the fantasy figure I lived in hopes of my mother becoming one day.

The time had come to face the truth—a thin blue line stared back at me. I had read the instructions so many times that I knew what it meant. *What am I going to do now? What if Mike doesn't want to know? What can I offer this baby?* All morning I rehearsed what to say to Mike. He had never talked about getting married or even living together. I hoped he would put his arms around me tell me everything was going to be fine and ask me to marry him, but I knew things like this never happened in real life. Abortion, as far as I was concerned, was not an option. Somehow, through my darkest times, something always turned up. I hoped my guardian angel was looking after me now.

Mike arrived to pick me up for a drive on the Moor. I would have to watch for the right moment. As we sat beside a small brook for a few hours, he kept asking me if I were OK. "You seem very quiet today."

"I have something to tell you. I'm pregnant," I blurted.

"Are you sure? I mean how do you know?" He sounded panicked.

"I took a home test. Mike, I need to know how you really feel."

He stood up with his back to me. Oh God! He's going to end our relationship! *How could I have been so stupid? Don't you dare show him how hurt you are!* I thought to myself. Push it down! Push it down deep! Don't show him you care! He sat back down beside me.

"What do you want to do about it?"

"I'll have an abortion if that's what you want," I answered, testing him.

"If that's what you want."

"Just leave it to me. Take me home!" I snapped.

I was trying to absorb his reactions. What did I expect? I felt so stupid and wished I had never met him. To be honest, I wonder if I slept with him that first night out of fear of losing him. I can't look after myself let alone provide for a baby! What a mess! Mike's silence was all the rejection I could cope with. I kept looking in his direction as he drove. *How could I have been so wrong?* I believed him every time he told me that he loved me. Now I won't see him anymore! No man will ever get close enough to me to do this again!

"Do you want to go see my sister? She may be able to help us."

"No. Just take me home! I don't want to see you anymore!"

"What do you mean?"

"You want me to get rid of it—don't you?"

"No! You were the one who said that! I just agreed with you! It's whatever you want to do."

"Exactly! And what I want is you out of my life! Stop the car! I'll walk!" I got out of the car and slammed the door with such rage that the passenger's side window shattered. He sped off and I marched along the road like a demonic idiot.

Why did I do that? What is wrong with me? I wanted to hit him yet he hadn't done anything. I was starting to resemble Mother with my cruelty toward Mike and my horrid spouting of words! Thoughts of me treating my own child the same frightened me! *What if I don't love the baby?* I had just thrown away the best thing that ever happened to me. I felt like getting drunk.

Mike had driven straight to Jane's house and explained the day's events. He was worried. He had witnessed outbursts from me before but said this was different. He had told his sister that he could not walk away; he loved me and was afraid of losing me.

I arrived home from my very long walk and was secretly glad to see Mike waiting in his car. And angry that he never came looking me. However, I was angrier with myself—the next time

I decide to scream at him and demand to get out of the car, I will make sure to be closer to my destination.

Mike and I talked and decided to rent a flat together. I wanted to be sure of him and needed to know that he was not going to turn into a monster once we were living together; I had to think about the baby. A good relationship was developing with Evie and Jim, I respected them enormously. Mike's dad was one of the few men I trusted. Mike and I talked about getting married. It was what I wanted more than anything, not just for me but also for our baby. I was an old-fashioned girl at heart and being married before the baby was born meant a lot to me. I wanted to keep the date of the wedding to ourselves because I didn't want anyone or anything spoiling it. We informed Evie and Jim just two days before.

"What do you mean, Saturday?" Jim asked, shocked.

"What about the reception? Let Jim and I help! Jane, Mike's sister will bake a cake and help prepare the food!" The bustle began.

Mike and I agreed to allow his parents to take charge of the reception; it was nice to belong to a family who cared. Our unborn child was going to have everything I never did. Then the dreaded words were spoken...

"When will we meet your parents, Sharon? We should meet them before the wedding."

I began to worry. How could I explain? I was getting on so well with Mike's family and this was going to spoil everything. If Jim believed Stepfather's version, my dreams of domesticity will be shattered.

Mike and I discussed my awkwardness. "You will have to tell your parents that we're being married. I'll go and see your parents. Perhaps this is the opportunity to make your peace, we'll both go together."

I refused to go to Mother's home. Mike volunteered and I was upset by his lack of understanding. To him, as with most other people, abuse is merely a word with imagined images—something equally easy to forget. To anyone who has lived through the trauma, it is an upsetting emotional experience with graphic pictures of the smallest distasteful details that are impossible to forgive.

I waited in his parents' garden for his return and was terrified he would come back with a different attitude toward me; convinced that I was overreacting, hysterical and lying to get attention. I knew Stepfather would probably tell Mike all manner of lies and mother would confirm them. When he returned he seemed excited as he explained that my parents were fine, that they would love to come to the wedding but, he said, I had to go and see them first.

"I'm not going on my own! You promise to stay with me at all times," I pleaded. Mike agreed. As I climbed into his car for the short journey to my past, I regretted agreeing to go. *What am I doing?* I wanted to hide within my own shell behind my safe walls and watch the events take place from a safe distance.

My heart was pounding with fear as Mike parked outside my parent's home. I feared what lay beyond the front door. Part of me hoped Mother would finally defend and protect me as she should have when I was a child and that my stepfather would be filled with remorse and no longer deny what he did to me. I wanted to be naïve and believe that there could be a fairytale ending. He would stop denying that he abused me—he had to, we both knew the truth. Now I had Mike to protect me and this gave me the courage I needed to walk toward the house but as we approached the front door, all the ghosts returned to life and instinct screamed at me to run. But I didn't—I had more to lose by not going in—the possibility of Evie and Jim doubting me as others did.

Stepfather opened the door and beckoned us in. I gripped Mike's arm and defiantly looked my stepfather in the eye—he was the one who lowered his head and couldn't look at me. He had not changed at all—his round face red from the day's boozing. Mother was in the living room. We were offered a cup of tea, which we declined and as I looked around the room, I saw that nothing had changed. Stepfather disappeared to putter around in the kitchen and Mike and mother were talking about the wedding. She had abused me physically and mentally over the years, but I believed she hated me most because she did not want to believe that her husband abused me.

Mother sat chatting to Mike like they were old friends. I knew her intention was to make me feel isolated and it was working. I looked around the room for some kind of memory of a happy time within these walls but echoes of bones breaking, pain, mistrust, sobs and screams were all I found. Whispers from the deepest crevices called to my soul as my body lurched with unseen hands fumbling, grasping at me, ready to take me back to the jaws of the beast. Stepfather appeared in the room and looked toward me. Alarm swept over me as the night devil winked with a knowing smirk on his face. He had taken off his shirt as he always did, his oversized belly hanging over the belt on his trousers. He was indeed an ugly person inside and out. I watched as he turned to go back in to the kitchen and it was as though he walked in slow motion.

I placed a protective hand over my unborn baby and terrors of yesteryears screamed through my spirit. I was in the night devil's den; the walls were shadowy and lifeless, surrounding the black hole of my past. *I must escape! I need to leave!* We made our excuses and left.

Back in the car, I was too angry to respond to Mike as he bantered on about my parents and how reasonable they were. Feelings of rage tore through me stronger than ever and it took all my strength and resources to control them. *Why are other people so blind to abusers? Why can't they see what their victims see? Who am I angrier with; Mike for believing they were normal people or my parents for making him believe they were normal people—or both?*

The day of the wedding arrived. Evie had done a wonderful job with the preparations. Mother, my stepfather and June attended, as did Mark and his family. Everything seemed to go well but I was not happy about Stepfather's presence. Oh, I smiled at the right times and did all the things as was expected of me, but I could not bring myself to relax. Stepfather had started to drink heavily. I became more afraid when Mother left early giving the excuse that she had to return to work. I knew she left for fear of the onslaught of fury bought on by Taff's alcohol intake. I was left with the one person I did not want there.

Jim, who had never said a detrimental word about anyone before, now made a comment about Taff's now loud and obnoxious behavior.

I asked Mark to try to get my stepfather to leave, which he managed to successfully accomplish somehow and I was finally able to relax. Mike's seventy-three-year young grandmother, who I had affectionately nicknamed Granny-bear, was the only one who saw through his parent-of-the-year act. "Who is that horrid man? Something is very deep and ugly about him," she stated matter-of-factly.

"He's my mother's husband."

"I'm so sorry! I didn't mean to be rude!"

"Don't worry, Granny-bear. I just wish everyone else had the same insight as you; the night devil is a chameleon."

The rest of my wedding day went well and the family that stayed and celebrated our union were all the family I would ever need.

Mike and I settled into family life very well. We were looking forward to our first Christmas together in our own little home and the birth of our first child; this happy event was due in January. Money was tight because I had given up work but we managed. Christmas was spent at the in-laws and was the best Christmas I had known with my own family.

I still wanted to find my real father and knew this would happen eventually, but I was not prepared for the struggle and heartbreak of it.

Christmas had come and gone and one day I was alone in the apartment. I had been feeling restless and decided to visit mother, something I had done a few times but always with Mike. I was also always careful to never be alone with Taff. Whenever I saw him, the child within me went into alarm and fear drained me of my ability to be the adult I was.

I left a note for Mike, requesting that he pick me up from Mother's house after work, then made my way to Mark's house. Lynda and I had a cup of tea and a chat; they now lived only a few houses away from mother. I waited until mother returned from work because it was Wednesday, her regular half-day off.

"You can take Steve with you, if you wish." Lynda offered. Steve was their son and growing into a very energetic little man and I loved him very much. Steve spent a lot of time with Stepfather and mother, something I could not understand my brother allowing.

"Come on Steve! Let's go to Nan's house!"

He was eager to go because he was overindulged by both of them. My baby would never stay overnight nor would I ever allow them to look after my child! Steve danced ahead as the warm January sun filtered through the clouds, he was already knocking on the back door when I entered the garden, which was unusual—the back door was never locked. Stepfather called from his bedroom window, "Hang on! I'll open the door."

"Where's mother?" I called up.

"Not home from work yet. She decided to stay in town."

"Leave it. I'll call back later." I could feel myself shaking! *Oh God! What am I going to do?* I did not want to be alone with him!

"You have bloody woken me now! Hang on, I'm coming down!" he barked.

I grabbed Steve and ordered him to stay with me as he wriggled to free himself. Stepfather appeared at the door and invited us in. I slipped onto a chair next to the back door and held onto Steve tightly. He kept trying to escape my lap—he preferred to play in the garden.

"Let him go. He can run around." Taff ordered.

I wanted to slap the little bugger as he willingly left me and headed for the garden. My mind raced for excuses to leave and I tried to think of something to say to hide my fear. *Was I overreacting?* Stepfather walked toward the door and I could feel my pulse racing as he stood watching Steve playing and was talking to him. Then he closed the door, complaining that he was cold, but I knew what was about to happen and I was terrified! *This is not going to happen!* I thought to myself and held a protective arm around my swollen belly; I felt my baby kicking inside.

"Open the door!" I demanded as I stood up. He started to snicker—it was the same mocking cackle he always used when he knew he was terrifying me. He had me cornered; I couldn't get past him and I feared him hurting my baby if he started to punch me.

"I'll ask you once more to open the bloody door!" All I could think about was my unborn baby. If he touched me, he would be soiling my baby as well and this baby was the one pure thing in my life, unspoiled by the filth I had survived. I was prepared to give my life to stop this from happening.

"So the little girl has grown. You think you're too big now?" he hissed demonically.

"Too big for you to handle!" I snapped back, scanning the room looking for something to use as a weapon, which I had no qualms about using. Slowly I eased myself away from him, trying to get as much distance as I could between us. I knew I couldn't get out the back door because he was standing next to it. Thoughts of escape raced through my mind and my head started to swim with utter terror. The front door was my only real option, but I would have to move fast. I would have to race through the front room and hope the front door was not locked and bolted. *Jesus, help stop this from happening!* I prayed. I abandoned the idea of bolting to the front door because I was too afraid of him catching me and beating me. I needed to protect my unborn child at all costs.

"Who do you think is going to believe you? No one did before and nobody will now." He was growling and snickering at the same time.

"I'll tell you who! Anyone who sees the bruises because you are going to have to kill me first! Open the fucking door, NOW!" Before anything else could be said, a knock on the door threw the fat bastard into a panic and I prepared to scream for help. My stepfather opened the door immediately; it was Steve.

"Why'd you lock me out?" he cried. I pushed past the night devil, grabbed Steve and walked out. I wanted to run, but did not want to give him the pleasure and satisfaction to see how much he had scared me. I was pleased with myself for standing up to him and wished I had the courage to have stood up to him a long time ago.

"You're back soon," Lynda observed. I wanted to tell her; desperate for someone just to comfort me, but knew no one would believe me. *How can one man be so evil and fool so many people?* I considered telling Mike but decided against reliving it. I decided it best to keep this to myself, to bury it deep. I may have won this battle but the war was still raging.

My due date came and went as I settled back into life once more. It had been two weeks since my recent escape from the night devil and I despised my lack of courage to report him. Once again, I started to make myself sick after meals and feelings of self-harm flowed through my every thought. I wanted to release the demons within my body. I felt physically sick and dirty, my blood seeped poison through my veins and I was desperate to watch it flow out of me, but I knew I needed to get a grip of my emotional stability for my baby's sake. I didn't know who to go to for help or how to explain why I felt so retched about myself.

I made my way to the local beach and sat watching the sea as the howling January winds whipped the tide, the white surf angry as she grappled with the sand, snatching it from the shores. I directed all my negative thoughts and feelings of betrayal into the grains of sand and watched as Mother Nature pulled them out to sea, forever lost in an ocean of salt. Cleansed and refueled, I made my way back home.

The hospital decided to induce my labor and Mike was by my side from the minute it started. The pain was unbearable! No one had prepared me for this and for the next twelve hours, my dignity no longer existed and instead I was little more than a nasty creature who spat wild innuendoes and utterly awful dialog at Mike. He patiently held my hand while I tried to break his fingers. I believed something was wrong. This is one of the most painful things anyone could do; no way was I ever having another baby!

I gave birth to a son at nine-thirty on the evening of January 20th, 1976. Mike was a proud and happy father of this bouncing baby boy. I was too tired and weak to muster the same enthusiasm.

I awoke the following morning to the nurses bringing all the babies in to the ward. I looked down at this helpless little infant placed in my arms and knew this was my son, but I did not feel like a mom—I was afraid of him. The nurse asked if I felt well enough to feed him.

"I'll give it a go."

"What's the baby's name?" the nurse inquired. I didn't have a clue what to name him. I would have liked to name him after my real father, but knew this would upset Mother.

I managed to feed him with the nurse's help and once they finally left me alone with him, I checked him over; two hands, ten fingers... and suddenly a wave of love toward this little person engulfed me! I realized then that I did not know how to show love to my son and I started to become upset. The nurse asked what was wrong, but I was too embarrassed to tell her.

She placed him in his crib and I couldn't take my eyes off him. He started to cry and again I picked him up and tried to comfort him without success. I felt the baby did not like me and this was his way of rejecting me.

"You must try to relax with him—he will sense your anxiousness. Give it time. Giving birth does not make you an instant mother," the nurse advised.

I knew too well that the nurse was right. I decided to have my shower, but then the baby started to cry again; the little bugger was starting to annoy me already. I wanted my bath, not to be here watching a screaming baby. I looked down at this helpless little human who instantly stopped crying when I picked him up, and as I cradled him in my arms, it felt awkward and cumbersome. I carefully placed him back in the crib and tiptoed toward the door, eager for my bath—and again he cried.

I was agitated by his attention-seeking and pulled at the handle of the door, sure if I let him cry he would eventually go to sleep. I stopped and listened to his heartfelt sobs and something inside pulled at my heart. I knew I should go and comfort him, but how? The truth was, I was afraid of him and the emotions he was stirring within me. I went back and pulled the curtains around my bed. Me and this little guy were now completely alone. I stroked his hair and examined every inch of him. He would rely on me for the most menial of tasks and to protect and nurture him.

"Hi I'm your mommy," I whispered as he nestled into me. I spoke to him gently and soothingly and meant every word I spoke to my son on this day.

"I am not always going to get it right, but I promise no one will ever hurt you. I will stand by you for the rest of your life. I will give my life to protect you, and there will be no secrets between us and no pain." This little boy was going to help me love again.

Mike arrived and we decided together that 'Barrie' was a fine name for this bonny little chap who had a mop of black hair and the smoothest of skin. I was in control of my eating habits and found motherhood exhausting but enjoyable. I still visited Mother occasionally, but having a child of my own made me question Mother's failure to protect and nurture me.

I would look at my child asleep in his cot and wonder how Mother could not have known what was going on? How could she allow the brutal beatings dished out by a drunken bully who was so insecure about himself that beating me senseless was how he derived his feelings of superiority? What a slime-ball! Looking to my past with a different attitude, I knew Mother lacked something inside of her to treat her child that way. How many times did she punch me in the face just for the fun of it? How could she have stood me in front of guests to belittle me constantly and make unfavorable comparisons between June and me about our appearances? I was the ugly duckling who was abused by both of them.

January the following year, a week before Barrie's first birthday, I gave birth to a second son. His arrival was just three minutes after reaching the hospital doors. Mike and I named him Paul. He was a very good baby, unlike Barrie who cried all day and night for the first twelve months; probably because I picked him up every second I could. I worried that he would feel lonely and unloved with Paul's arrival. Barrie was the baby I grew with, who taught me how to love and to accept love. Paul was also a beautiful baby and I fretted at times that somehow I would lose this little family of mine.

My relationship with Mike weathered some stormy seas and I went through terrible turmoil, wondering if I could trust him with our sons. Would I know if he were abusing them? Unjustly, I would snap if he raised objections to Barrie's crying or dare to say anything derogatory about his lack of sleep.

Mike decided with our expanding family that he needed to get a better paying job and applied with a factory on the outskirts of town. He was accepted immediately. I was happy with my little brood—having my own children made me feel complete.

I had worried about my feelings toward a second child; I loved Barrie completely and intently, my instincts to protect him unyielding; I feared not being able to feel the same depths of love for my second son, but as I held him in my arms for the first time, the overwhelming love I had for Barrie was present straight away for my second little man. I could not contemplate life without either of them and would often sit beside their cots while they slept. The overwhelming love I had for them would consume me with fear, constantly wondering when it would all be taken away.

We were offered a brand-new house with three bedrooms from our local authority and jumped at the opportunity as it was only a short walk from Mike's new job. It snowed the day we moved into it and I found out I was pregnant—again. The biggest surprise was that I was four months pregnant! We joked we would have one baby a year for the first five years of marriage. I worried about our finances and how three extra little people were draining all we had. My home was sparely furnished but, clean, so clean it squeaked at times from the constant polishing and washing of all I owned. Looking back I now realize it was my way of coping with the mixed-up emotional cyclone of yesteryears spinning in turmoil waiting for the exit to open. All that pent-up emotions has to be released.

On the new estate, there were many young families and gossip about one family in particular were rife; the mother was known to like a drink and was feared by many, her reputation spread like wildfire.

As I was walking to the shops, I bumped into an old school friend, Bobbi Joe. We were excited to have found each other again, although her presence brought many memories flooding back as she laughed and joked about our school days with fondness. Bobbi was raising her daughter alone and I admired her determination. We rekindled our friendship and once again grew close. Bobbi was the only one who could tell me if I were wrong, she was always honest and it was this quality that I admired the most about her.

While sitting in my garden one evening and watching the children playing, I noticed a man looking at me. He walked toward the garden gate and called, "You're Sharon Arscott, aren't you?"

"I haven't used that name in a few years," I laughed.

It was Adam, an old school chum. He had not changed at all and even had the same haircut. I remember all the girls fancied him—and many fought over him. The only thing different was that his voice seemed deeper. I felt uncomfortable meeting anyone again from my childhood or the neighborhood of my youth. I was unsure if they knew of my allegations, which had faded unspoken between Mother, Stepfather and myself. He invited me over for a coffee, explaining he was married with three children and lived two streets away. I said I would try to visit later that evening when Mike came home from work. I was surprised how many people from my school days lived on the estate and how many remembered me fondly. I had always believed I was hated by most people and my school days were never memories I had cherished.

About eight o'clock that evening, I asked Mike if he minded me going out for an hour. After putting the children to bed, I walked to Adam's house and knocked on the door. A woman about my age invited me in and introduced herself as Amy, Adam's wife. I could see she had been drinking alcohol, which made me nervous; I didn't like being around people who were drunk—they were too unpredictable. Three young children ran around the house, anarchy at its best! They did not seem affected by their mother's condition in the least. A voice from the lounge shouted, "Hello!" It was Adam and he was just as drunk as his wife. I was mortified and wanted to leave but worried about offending them.

"Want a drink?"

"Yes, tea please," I responded.

"No! A proper drink!" Amy heckled me.

"No, thanks. I don't drink very much."

"Are you saying that I do?"

"Cut it out, Amy," Adam coaxed as he entered the room.

Whoosh! She hit him in the face! I ran out of the house and did not stop until I reached Bobbi's home and banged on her door! I panicked thinking Amy could have followed me.

"For Christ's sake, where's the fire?" I heard Bobbi shouting as she opened the door. I pushed past her, my breathing heavy. My large pregnant body shaking with adrenalin as my lungs felt as though they would explode with this sudden burst of activity. I grasped a cigarette, lit it and drew on it hard. Coughing and spluttering, my breathing erratic through my choking, I tried to explain to Bobbi who was wide-eyed watching me gag on my own words.

"You will never guess what's just happened!" I told Bobbi-Joe everything; I was calm about it now, but was nearly crying when it had happened. Bobbi then told me they were the family everyone was gossiping about. Amy had recently lost a baby boy born with a heart defect. The surgeons could not help him, so they sent him home to die. Three weeks later, he died in Amy's arms.

I held my own tummy and could feel my baby moving. I wouldn't know how to deal with a situation like that and I was ashamed with myself for reacting like I had.

"You can't help people like that," Bobbi added, "unless they ask for help themselves."

"Bobbi, I don't believe we have the right to judge."

"I've seen that look before. Stay out of it. They are bad news."

"I'm not likely to go there again! I am more afraid of Amy hitting me; she fights like a man!"

"And you don't Sharon? Look what you were like at school! No one dared to bully you! Nope! I think she should be the one who's worried, not you."

"You were no pushover either! I think I should go and tell Amy you want to be her friend!"

We chatted and teased each other like schoolkids. In the early hours of that morning, the telltale signs of impending labor coursed through my body. My labor lasted two hours, which took everyone by surprise. The baby was in the breach position and that's the way he entered the world. I worried about the other two children and the effect of having less of Mommy's attention. I secretly would have liked a girl, but when I looked into the beautiful blue eyes of my third son, I wouldn't swap him for all the little girls in the world.

Three babies, all less than four years old! My days were busy, my nights were exhausting but I was relishing in the role of housewife and mother! I had three little men whom I adored, I was the center of their world and they were the center of mine. The new addition to our family was named James after his Grandfather. I respected my in-laws immensely and would do anything for them.

Our family became very close with an older woman who lived next door. Her name was Maria and she often popped in for a cup of tea and a chat. She would also help with the children. I was a very protective mother and had made a promise to each child when born that they would never live in fear of their father or me. As much as I loved Mike, I would not tolerate abuse of our children. I also had a great understanding of behavior and patience with people and that sometimes drove Mike mad.

Mike and I had a good marriage and I was more able to show him my true feelings as time passed. He was as quiet and unobtrusive and I was outgoing and sometimes loud. I could walk into a room and instantly make friends whereas Mike was happy to demure. This does not mean in any way that he was weak, he was the stronger one—the rock—he just did not feel the need to prove it as often as I did.

I visited Mother on a few occasions, which also meant that I saw my stepfather; I was uncomfortable with this contact, but I tolerated it only for her sake because I no longer needed her approval as much as I had a few years back. James would soon be one year old—he was growing into an inquisitive little fellow. Barrie and Paul were good kids and both were out of nappies and clean, even though they had just turned three and two respectively.

The old familiar signs were overtaking me again as I cleaned my teeth after yet another bout of morning sickness. Mike was going to have his own room, he joked.

I bumped into Adam on my way to the doctor's office. He apologized for his behavior the last time we met. It had been fifteen months or so and I had all but forgotten about it. I inquired about Amy and he lowered his head, explaining things were fine but his body language said differently. We parted company and I continued happily on to see the doctor without giving it a second thought.

A few months later, an appointment was made for me to attend the local hospital because my weight had declined and the doctor was worried. I was not about to explain my bulimic episodes to him. I was not only embarrassed, but also afraid I would lose my children if the authorities knew. Today though, we were seeing our baby with a new imaging machine. Mike and I were very excited as we chatted about life in general and our growing family. I climbed onto the bed and the radiologist squirted a cold, sticky gunk all over my stomach, explaining that the pictures were created by sound waves. This meant nothing to me! I was in total awe to see my baby inside the womb.

"There's the baby's head, Mrs. Wallace. There's the spine and his little feet and toes. Oh look! He's sucking his thumb!"

Mike and I tried to muster the same enthusiasm, but to be honest all we saw was a blob of grey and black. We asked about the use of the word 'he' that she bantered around so easily but the radiologist explained all the babies were referred to as he, and that it was impossible to predict the baby's gender.

Mike had been working the night shift for some time and I was getting used to being on my own, not that I had much time for myself. I heard a knock at the front door and I answered it, startled to see that it was Amy and she was very drunk. I ushered her into the dining room, not wanting the children to witness her condition.

"I won't be a minute!" I excused myself after sitting her down at the table. "I am just getting the children off to bed." I rushed back upstairs and quickly got them into their beds and settled for the night, all the time wondering why she had visited.

"Would you like a cup of tea?" I asked nervously.

"No, I don't drink it," she replied.

Slumping against the wall, I tried to make small talk and prayed one of my friends would call. I could see her aggressive attitude had been a mask and her pain from the loss of her child was still very raw. We had been talking for some time before Amy finally mentioned the baby. I listened intently to all she had to say and I became more convinced that the aggression was a cover, a disguise she wore well to conceal her pain.

It was nearing midnight and I was hoping she would go home soon. A knock on the front door had me totally perplexed; who could be calling at such a late hour? It was Adam. I was relieved to see him because he would take Amy home and I could have my home to myself again.

"Come in," I almost pleaded, pointing toward the dining room. He stooped down and soothingly said, "Come on my love, it's time to go home."

Amy had fallen asleep and he was gently waking her. She swung out and hit him with such force that the poor man fell backward and bounced off the radiator.

"Get lost!" she screamed at him. "You fuck!"

This time I did get involved. *Not in my house! I won't have this!* If these two want to fight, fine. Mike and I had never allowed the children to witness any form of aggression. Adam got up and left. Great, I thought; now what do I do? Amy started to go on about her baby in a drunken drool of self-pity. I told her to stop being so selfish and reminded her of their other children at home. They were not dead! They were very much alive and needed her! Drinking was not solving her grief, just masking it. I snapped my mouth shut as I realized what I had said and to whom. *Here we go*, I thought, *now I get hurt!* Instead, she walked out of the house without speaking a word.

A couple of days later, I was sweeping the back garden when Barrie excitedly rushed to me, someone was knocking on the front door. I opened the door and a deliveryman smiled as he handed me a bowl of fruit—the card read simply: "Thanks, Amy and Adam."

Later, Amy explained that no one had spoken to her like I had and it was the shock she needed. Everyone would cross the street rather than talk to her. *I wonder why?* I mused. This was the beginning of a long and close friendship.

If Only Someone Spoke For Me.

Little girl who lays so still,
little girl whose words are nil.
Speak to me beyond your silence,
help me create your story of violence.
Little girl your age is three,
I see the marks and bruises on thee.
Silent eyes closed, screwed tight,
to hide the terror that was caused this night.
Whirling from the saw will describe,
the last few hours before you died.
Broken ribs are exposed and viewed.
I write down all your injuries—old and new.
Little girl whose body is small,
no weight to help when blows were drawn.
Daddy and mummy will fight who is wrong,
but I will recreate your sad songs.
Little girl sleep well tonight,
the autopsies done you will win this fight.
Guilt exposed wrongdoers will pay,
for beating and starving you for thirty-one days.
Little girl all swathed in white,
sit with the angels feel warmth this tonight.

6 The Truth is Always Sitting on Simmer

Motherhood became my daily chore—it defined me. I was learning every day about babies and their little idiosyncratic personalities. Being a mother changed every aspect of me for the better, there was no limit to what I would do to protect my boys. My thoughts and feelings of love toward them were all consuming; they had my love forever.

Our fourth son was born in March 1980 and we named him Michael, after his father; he was the cutest little man I had ever seen.

In October 1981, I gave birth to another son, Christopher. He was a bonny, bouncing little man but because he would be my last child, he was a little special to me. I settled with my five boys into a daily routine of nappies, bottles and mischief. I worried constantly about my parenting skills and was always afraid of being judged. I also wanted my children to feel safe and loved and tried hard to show them every day. These five little men of mine had the most mixed-up mommy and deserved better. At times, my past arose and invaded the most simplistic of things in my everyday life. I struggled at times to be the mother my children deserved but ultimately, I did many things wrong. I tried desperately to prove I was not the psychotic monster that Mother and Stepfather portrayed me as to others.

Barrie was starting his first term at infant's school and I think I was more affected than he was. I stood at the school gate for an hour making sure he was settled and did not run out. The head teacher approached and asked me to leave because it was unsettling for him. I walked home feeling an immense sense of loss. I was to relive this day four more times and the hardest to let go of was my youngest, Christopher. Once he was in school, the house became too quiet.

Mike's health was starting to concern me. He went through periods where his loss of balance affected his ability to walk. He experienced weakness in the legs and arms and confusion at times. He sought medical advice and was simply issued tablets for stress. I still had issues to deal with and my childhood demons were never far, always simmering just below the surface. I had never had counseling and although I saw Mother at times, my stepfather was always present. I don't know how I managed to be in the same room with him—I had to close the pictures down and ignore my emotions toward him.

We were offered a four-bedroom home and with our growing family we simply couldn't refuse. The house was only four doors away and so I was able to maintain the friends I had made. We all settled into the house and the extra space was a welcome. I made the children a den under the stairs and James played for many hours in his own little make-believe world. I was invited in a few times and I remembered the magical time in the attic of one of the orphanages I had stayed in during my early childhood. This little den was an aircraft, a cave, a car and even a forest—their enthralling imaginations were unlimited and released.

I had started work in a local factory on the night shift and Mike had changed his job and was now a taxi driver. Money was tight as Mike's health problems went from mild to severe. I was worried for Mike and angry about the doctor's suggestion that it was psychosomatic.

As the weeks went by, I worked hard to bring in extra money but could not trust anyone to look after the children. I worked until seven in the morning and Mike would have the children up and ready for school. The three oldest were in school, which left the two babies, Michael Jr. and Christopher, who we affectionately called Gripper, home with me. I would sleep when they napped in the mornings and again when Mike returned from work at five thirty. I started work at nine p.m. so it gave me a few hours of sleep, but it took its toll on all of us. When I fell down the stairs and broke my ankle, I realized how affected the children were by my absence. After healing, I decided not to return to work.

I awoke to the phone shrilling out one lazy Saturday morning. It was Mother calling to inform me that she was moving to a house near ours. I dropped the receiver in disbelief and shock! *Why would she want to move closer?* I did not want Taffy living near me! It was bad enough just seeing him on the few occasions I visited Mother.

Mother moved into the estate and I began seeing her more often. Taffy disappeared to the pub every day and Mother would walk to my house. I could tolerate her company at times and we started to talk more. Sometimes she would get a little spiteful toward me, but I said nothing—I knew she was still upset about my accusations against her husband. It was not long until the conversation turned to my biological father. I asked as many questions as I could think of and she seemed eager to answer them. I soaked up all she had to say. I made my way into town the following morning to check every Arscott across the country and if I failed, I would start on the electoral register.

I was surprised to find a person who seemed like a match in name and even the area of his last known address. Excitedly, I scribbled down the information and also found another set of Arscotts that were possibly my grandparents. I dialed the number as soon as I arrived home. I felt awkward when a gentleman answered, and I asked if he were Peter Arscott and if he had a daughter? He replied, "Yes," and I had no doubts that the man on the other end of the phone was my biological father. An unsettling quietness stood between us as I tried to find something to say, but the words were few from both of us. His reaction was not as I had dreamed all these years.

I suggested that I phone back later to give us both time to absorb the moment and he agreed. As I cradled the receiver, I realized I had just spoken to a man I had placed on a pedestal all my life. I had visions of him loving me as a father should and holding me while I relayed my terrible childhood; feelings of being loved and comforted by him as only a father could, clouded my mind—I could only see love, acceptance and peace.

I waited a few hours and then phoned him back, but was able to speak only to his wife. She said that he had gone to work and would phone me on the weekend. We spoke for a while and she seemed nice and was interested in my little family. As the weekend approached, I informed my brother Mark and Mother that I had spoken to my father. Mark was weary and advised that if he had wanted to see us he could have easily sought us out, as I had him. Mother was neutral and gave no opinion—not that hers would have been heard. I had blinders on when it came to my dad! I had wanted this for most of my life and no one was going to stop me.

I dialed his number, trembling with anticipation of hearing his voice, but was informed once again that he was away working. His wife asked many questions and over the weeks, she phoned me but I was never able to speak to Dad. Mother filled in the gaps for me, informing me that he really was not a nice person and was doing as he always did, hiding away and letting others converse for him.

"He probably knows I've told you everything and thinks you are after his money," Mother spitefully informed me. Images of the beatings she administered resurfaced in my mind as she ranted about how much like him I was and how uncanny the resemblance was.

I tried many times to speak to him; I would have fallen on my knees and begged him to accept me. His rejection tore at my heart! I was depressed by the rejection and my children were all that stopped me from falling into deep despair.

"He doesn't want to know you, Sharon! You were his bastard daughter! I told you before, what a coward he was!" Mother's poisonous words stabbed into my heart, tearing me open like a knife. I could see she delighted in my pain and reaction and loved the dismal storm in which I now walked. I stopped trying to talk to him after a few months, but told Mother the opposite. I deliberately led her to believe that I had spoken to him many times, that he had in fact invited me to his home and I was leaving that weekend. A fantasy life with my father was born and I had many conversations and experiences with him—or so Mother believed.

Stepfather had the audacity to phone me to say that Mother was devastated that I was now involved with a man who had never done anything for me. I was angry that this abuser dared to condemn me for upsetting her. I added more lavish images the next time I spoke with Mother. I could see how upset she had become. However, it was not because I had met or spoken with my father. Rather, it was because she believed my stories and thought he had fared so much better in life than her and now she was afraid that Father would find out how wicked she had been. I found out years later about the true circumstances of my brothers and I being placed in the orphanage. Oh parents of mine! When first we set out to deceive!

I settled back into life with my young family and gradually stopped speaking of my father but kept in contact with my grandparents, who were lovely people. I felt sad for the loss of our relationship and although we met, I felt no kinship with them. My grandmother was a sturdy lady, my grandfather a gentleman; he had served in the armed forces and served as an officer.

I reflected with grandma a memory of when I was 12 years old and they had made arrangements to visit us at Mother's home. I was going to tell them about my stepfather and ask them to rescue me from my prison. Mother made us sit all day in the lounge waiting for their arrival and I was devastated when they did not turn up. I recalled sitting all day and watching the hands of the clock move from ten in the morning to four in the afternoon. Grandma remembered that Mother had refused to allow them to visit and had even refused to give them our address. I was starting to see how Mother could have been mentally ill. Mother had beaten me severely that day because I had cried when grandma and grandpa did not turn up.

I did not discuss this with Mother, but my attitude was changing and I believe she felt it. I decided to tell my grandparents the truth about my childhood, which up until now, they believed was an idyllic life. As I wrote the letter, I think I secretly hoped they would tell my father and he would then contact me. I still hoped he would acknowledge and comfort me. Soon after, my Grandma died and if ever I needed proof that I was not included as a member of the Arscott family, I got it when I was not invited to the funeral because "it would be too awkward for my biological father." I wanted to scream at those people! I may not have been around when I was young, but I was just as much family as they were and the same blood flowed through my veins as did theirs. I was shattered beyond consolation when I hid in my bedroom and cried for hours, the rejection hurt as much as any pain I had ever experienced.

I decided then that I would never try to contact my father again. Before she died, grandmother had disclosed to me that my father had shamed her with his rejection of his own children. My grandparents had wanted to adopt all of us, but father insisted we be placed in a home with the option of adoption. Grandmother had kept all correspondence from the children's home over the years. It was nice to know that someone had fought to keep me and that my grandparents wanted to raise me at one time. It had been at my father's insistence that I was to be kept estranged from the family and my fate was sealed. Now, this chapter in my life was over...or so I thought.

Maria, my neighbor and friend, knocked on my door—she was excited and insisted that she had something important to talk about. She told me that Mother had stopped her as she walked her dog and had invited her in for a cup of tea. She said that Mother had spilled the details of my accusations against her husband and also told a story about a daughter Mike and I had who was taken away from us. I listened intently and was dumbfounded about why mother should lie about such a heinous crime—what did she hope to accomplish? Maria continued to explain how my daughter was nearly killed by Mike's hand. Mother had said that Mike beat her unconscious when she was two years old.

I waited for Maria to laugh and declare she was only joking, April Fools, or something, but her face was serious and her eyes were brimming with tears. I snatched up the phone and called Mother immediately to ask her what kind of game she was playing. She denied even seeing Maria at all. I looked over to Maria, sitting in my kitchen and knew she was not the liar Mother implied she was. I put down the phone and explained to Maria that the accusations I made were true but we had never had a daughter and that Mother had denied even seeing her. I knew Maria was not making up stories and that Mother was playing her mind games as usual. She was trying to punish me for being in contact with my father, or so mother thought.

Word spreads fast on housing estates and many people looked to the ground when I approached, believing I had an abused daughter—apparently Mother's tongue wagged over-time. My anger would erupt and I became aggressive to anyone who approached me for the smallest of things. My reputation preceded me. My three oldest boys went to the park with Margi, one of only three people I trusted with my young brood. On their return, I had tea ready and their baths run. They sat at the table eating and talking excitedly about their adventure in the park when James, my very inquisitive four-year-old informed me that I was a liar. Shocked by his remark, I asked why he thought this. He said Nanny Davies had been in the park and told him that his mommy tells lies. Barrie tried to hush James up and uneasily played with his food.

I sensed his discomfort and reassured him that Mommy was not angry with him and had them tell me everything, reminding my sons that secrets were not good. I was not prepared for the story about to be unfolded by my four-year-old. He used words he did not know the meaning of and asked what sex meant. My rage was immense but my reaction was controlled as I laughed and joked with my children and tried to ease their frustrations caused by thoughts in their heads that no one had the right to place in them. I phoned Margi and asked her to come to the house. After I bathed my children and made sure they put no importance to the day's events, I spoke to Margi. She claimed to be unaware of the conversation between James and Mother. Although Mother was at the park, Margi never actually spoke to her. I asked Margi to watch the children while I went to mother's home.

I was ready to do battle, I could take whatever Mother dished out to me, but I would not sit back and watch my children get emotionally abused with her venomous lies. I sharply knocked on Mother's door and as she opened it I pushed past her.

"Where is he?"

I wanted to face Stepfather with the accusations at last because this had gone as far as it was going! Mother informed me that he was at the pub and would not be back until late evening. Thinking back now, I believe she was lying because I have never known him to go to the pub in the evenings. I often wonder where he was that day and know that blood would have been spilled if not mine—then his. I shouted at her for involving my children in her cruel games and made her aware that I was their mother and I would do whatever needed to keep them safe! If she ever approached them again with her vile accusations, I would physically hurt her if need be! I left mother's home slamming the door behind me in a thunderous crash.

Returning home, my pulse raced adrenaline throughout my body! I calmed myself down and began to wonder when my stepfather would arrive to confront me with his drunken belligerence. I was ready to do battle tonight; this momma bear had been riled! I sat watching my sons playing in the lounge and realized for the first time how innocent I was in all my stepfather had done to me. I should have been protected by Mother, not punished. I deserved a better life than the one I had with them! I was a victim of both their rages and dysfunctions. I slipped into the kitchen to hide my tears as I realized just how retched mother really was. James appeared by my side and tugged on my shirt, "Mommy? Is you all right? Why are you sad?"

How could I explain to this precious little fellow that the world is sometimes cold and cruel and that his nana was a nasty, mean, woman who used him and his brothers to hurt me?

"Mommy got soap in her eye," I lied. I sat tense and ready until midnight but no one came.

I was awakened early in the morning to the sound of the doorbell. I looked to my bedside clock to see it was only six thirty a.m. I jumped out of bed and looked out the window to see who my early visitor was. It was Mother! I had calmed down since last night but the old stomach-churning feeling quickly returned as I opened the door to her.

"I have one question to ask and I want the bloody truth!" Mother angrily ordered. I asked her to wait while I returned the children upstairs—I did not want them to witness our conversation.

"Ok, Ask!" I demanded when I returned to the front room. I felt uneasy and afraid, exactly as I did as a child.

"Did he do what you accused him of?"

I was taken aback by her frankness and could see by her eyes that she wanted me to say I had lied and for an instance, I nearly did.

"He did it all Mom—and more," I heard myself reply. The scenario bizarre, the conversation emotionless. I had played this scene over and over in my mind for many years, but there was no hugging and kissing, no apologies, no comforting and making it all better; there were just cold words between us.

"I knew it! I thought there was something going on."

I looked to mother as fury tore through me. "You knew? You had an *idea*? What the fuck are you saying to me, Mother?"

"I noticed a few times when my bed was empty and I heard him leaving your room," she began.

"Get out of my house! I have lived a lifetime being called a liar and now you say you knew?" I opened the front door and demanded that she leave immediately; screaming at her until I thought the veins in my throat would burst.

"I wanted to be sure," she protested.

"Fucking get out, mother! You will never be sure! Did he? Didn't he? Did she? Didn't she? Welcome to my world, you bitch!"

I slammed the door behind her and fell to the floor. I couldn't believe that all my adult life I had tried to make up for the pain I believed I had caused her when all along, she was punishing me because her husband was a pedophile.

Inevitably, my children had heard the terrible words between us and as they rushed to me, I embraced their comfort. "Nanny is a bitch!" James declared. I tried to explain to them that Nanny was angry with me and not them but I failed my children on this day and had no strength to make amends. Mother left the estate a few months later and finally divorced Stepfather.

Our lives were about to get more complicated as Mike's health deteriorated and his ability to work was impaired. We had purchased our home and the mortgage hard to maintain. I knew the stress was making him worse. He was a proud man and a good one and watching his family go without was hard on him. I tried to maintain a normal routine for the children's sake but knew the time was fast approaching when the house would be taken from us. Mike and I never realized this was just a hiccup compared to what we were about to face.

Beaches

Wind in my hair sand on my feet what more can I ask, when troubles are deep

Save yourself no one to rely to pick you up, and stop you cry.

Many times when I sink too low, the beach is the only place I know.

I can dream; lose myself in the surf this will ease the painful hurt.

Clouds fluffy drifting high pick me up before I die.

Lay on the beach covered in sand at last I'm alone, imagination in hand.

There's no pain just the sound of the gulls, building nests to nurture their young.

Free from stress and memory of pain, I gather my strength to start again.

7   Fighting My Own Insanity

Mike had been home from work for two months and the mortgage unpaid. We had the bailiffs knocking on the door and the decision was made for Mike to declare bankruptcy. He was terribly ashamed—especially when it appeared in the local paper. I felt no shame at all. Our house was just brick and mortar to me; my home was wherever Mike and the children were. I was happy as long as we were together and had our health. I scanned the papers looking for private accommodation but it was difficult to find any that would accommodate or accept us with five sons. Intolerance arose instantly when I revealed how many children were involved; the youngest, Gripper, was seven and the oldest, Barrie, was now thirteen.

Mike had just returned home from taking the children to school and I was packing some more clothes and waiting for a phone call from yet another potential landlord when the phone shrilled out and I eagerly picked up the receiver and listened. Someone was hysterical and was frantically telling me to go and get the children! For a few seconds I couldn't make sense of the conversation until I heard Mark say, "Lynda's dead! I've been arrested for murder! Get my kids!"

I passed the phone over to Mike as Mark continued on frantically. I was unable to absorb our conversation; I believed he was winding us up but when I heard Mike promise to do as requested before he replaced the receiver and seeing his ashen face, I knew Mark was serious and that we had to hurry.

I thought I was dreaming and someone would wake me from this nightmare as we drove to Mark and Lynda's home. A policeman stood at their front door and refused to allow us in when we arrived. I explained that we had come to pick up the children but he told us unequivocally that further questions would not be tolerated, that the children were not in the house. Their children—Rupert was eight months old, Lucy was nine and Steve was now eighteen. I searched the neighborhood for them and eventually found the baby at a house across the road. The poor little guy was fretful and crying for his mommy. I held him to me and wondered how we were going to manage. We had to leave our house in six weeks and it was already hard enough finding a home to rent with our own five children. I had no idea how long we would have my brother's children. We learned that Lucy had gone to the police station to see her dad so we made our way there to pick her up. I was concerned about how she would react about staying with us as I had not been close to Mark since leaving Plymouth fifteen years earlier. We had kept in touch but it was always tense. I had no time to think about Lynda's death or the circumstances that led to Mark's arrest; all I could think about were the children, caring for them and worrying about how they were affected.

We parked outside the police station and as Mike and I walked toward the entrance, I asked if he would back me with any decisions I made pertaining to Mark's children.

"Of course, whatever you feel is best, but Mark will be home soon," he assured me as he placed a strong arm around me although I felt the weakness in his gait as we entered the building. Lucy was with Steve and refused to leave until she saw her daddy. She was a determined little girl with a spirit that was unperturbed by recent events.

The officer on desk-duty explained that Mark would be interviewed once a doctor deemed him fit. We eventually talked

Lucy into coming home with us and Steve was going to stay with his girlfriend's family. Once home, we quickly rearranged sleeping quarters to accommodate everyone, but the baby would not settle with anyone other than Lucy.

The welfare people arrived just as my own children were coming home from school. I would have preferred having a chance to explain the day's events to them first. I was terrified they would be taken and placed in care—especially when they realized we were losing our home. My life was turned inside out for the next few days. The police wanted to question Lucy about the night her mommy died and I was not allowed to be there. I did notice that she became withdrawn after her interview; she seemed to shut down emotionally about her mother's death.

Mother, whom I had not seen since the day we talked about my stepfather twelve months before, arrived at my home with June. The police interviewed her upstairs in my bedroom and asked her about Mark and Lynda's relationship. I listened as she told them that Mark had a temper and she had often stepped in to calm the situation. Yes, Mark had used violence in the past toward Lynda. Yes, he had hit the children. Yes, in her opinion, too hard at times. I couldn't believe the answers Mother gave and was angry that she could sit and offer disparaging judgments about Mark and his home life—especially when he needed his family the most.

In truth, Mark and Lynda had stopped seeing mother eighteen months previous, but even before that, mother never visited their home. Mother left after she gave her scathing statement and I felt I had to try to repair the damage caused by her callous lies when the police interviewed me. I told them everything about our past and answered every question as honestly as I could, but sometimes I worried that my answers could incriminate Mark worse. I worried that any talk of violence could be damning to him.

Lynda's sister, Beth, phoned and accused Mark of murder. I did not know how to respond, I hadn't spoken to Mark so I knew nothing about what had transpired that night. I didn't know if he was guilty or innocent. But I was sure of one thing, if Mark had a hand in Lynda's death then it was not intentional. Lucy spoke to Beth and passed me the phone when their conversation had finished. She covered the mouthpiece and whispered that she did not want to go and stay with her Aunt Beth. I tried to convey this to Beth but she was too distraught to listen. She unjustly accused me of manipulating the children against her and slammed the phone down. I felt afraid to say or do anything without the full story from Mark. But I do know I would be determined and loud when it came to the welfare of my brother's children. After all, I knew better than most how manipulative adults can be and I feared Beth's anger. Grief would be misplaced upon the children if they stayed with her. Everyone needed time to encompass the situation and the terrible loss of a member of the family, made worse by her young age and the unanswered questions surrounding her death.

I was finally allowed to see Mark the following day. The police were concerned about his mental wellbeing so his cell door was left open and an officer stationed outside his cell at all times for fear he would try to commit suicide. I was stunned by his appearance. He was truly a broken man; his breath reeked and his clothes were disheveled and dirty. He cried in my arms like a baby and it took all my strength to stay strong for him. I wanted to cup him in my hands and take him home. This was my big brother, but now he was only a shell of the man I knew.

Mark sobbed over the night's events when Lynda died. He had to deal with being arrested and worry about the future of his children, mourning her death had been overshadowed. He said that Lucy had found her but that he was also worried about Steve because he was in the home as well. He made me promise to look after them and not allow anyone else to take them. It was difficult to leave him there and as I walked away, I knew I would do all I could to help him. I know he was not there for me when I needed him most, but we were kids then—now we are adults and able to control our own lives and choices. Our children relied on us, so I was not about to allow my niece and nephew to be taken and placed in a home. History was not going to be repeated.

Mike's brother Dan had a house he rented to students and offered it to us, providing we paid the rent. We accepted gratefully. My brother was released on bail after a week and a date was scheduled for his appearance before the local magistrate. He was bailed to mother's home but I requested that our home be used as a second address, knowing it would not work out for him to be living with her. I was adamantly against Lucy staying with Mark at mother's home because although mother had divorced Taff, they still remained friends and Stepfather was a regular visitor to mother's house. Although no one believed me, I knew the truth and she needed to be protected from him—and I would do whatever it took to keep Lucy safe. Mark was preoccupied with grief and I knew vulnerability was an opening my stepfather would use, given half the chance.

Mike, six boys, one girl and I set up residence in a rented house with the future unknown. We settled into somewhat normality, but the recent additions and the loss of our home was having some negative effects on my lads, especially Gripper. He resented Rupert and the extra attention I needed to give the baby. After yet another tantrum and jealous words toward Rupert, I knew I had to do something; Gripper was the baby of the family and was finding it hard adjusting to having a younger guest in the house, demanding his mommy's attention. I assured Gripper that all of them were my babies and no matter how old, or how many children I have, they were all special. I reassured him that although Rupert was a baby and needed special attention, Gripper was—and always will be—my baby. Gripper soon began to relax and started to play with Rupert and even helped me feed and bathe him.

The rest of the family had problems with Lucy because they thought she would get preferential treatment because she was a girl. We all faced some trying times but we eventually found a way to live together harmoniously. Lucy still showed signs of bereavement. It had been three months since Lynda had died but her funeral had still not been arranged and Mark was still unable to face going back into their home. A few months before Lynda's death, they had decided to buy a new house and the mortgage had been arranged; all Mark needed to do was find a house—but he lost interest after his wife's death.

The day arrived for his court appearance and the mass of people who came to support him was overwhelming. The courtroom was packed from wall to wall with people and the double entry doors were left open as people waited in the corridors. My brother and sister-in-law were well known among the dart players of Plymouth. The coroner testified that Lynda had died of an embolism that ruptured in her neck. Mark was released without charge and Lynda's body was finally released, five months after her passing and her funeral finally arranged.

I was quite worried about Lucy's inability to express her feelings about her mother's death. She had not shed a tear and seemed to hide her feelings behind a mask of laughter. At Lynda's funeral, Mark was grief-stricken beyond words and as we drove behind the hearse, Lucy and Steve hung onto Mark and tried to comfort him. I watched as this little girl acted like an adult and wondered what was going on in her young mind. At home later that evening, Lucy's behavior became bazaar as she loudly shrieked at the boys and made her presence unmistakably known to everyone.

I took her aside to speak about Lynda. I tried to explain that it was all right to cry. She could scream, shout, laugh, cry or whatever made her feel better inside—that she needed to express her feelings and release them. We stood in the garden that night and Lucy finally screamed until she was hoarse. Eventually, she told me about the night her mommy died. She had been taken to her nana's house and while she sat on the stairs weeping, she was told to be quiet because her crying was upsetting others. That night Lucy buried her tears; afraid her expression of grief would upset the family. I took Lucy into the garden and we both screamed until we were hoarse. This little girl was a brave soul and had just started the road to healing.

Mark looked for another home but when the insurance company refused him the money and cited his arrest for Lynda's death as the reason, he simply accepted their decision and looked for rental accommodation instead. I was angry that they dared to use Lynda's death as an excuse to stop payment, so with Mark's permission, I set about to challenge the decision. After a few months, he received all the money due to him, purchased his new three-bedroom home and had his children back. We stayed close for many years after and I fought in my brother's corner on several occasions. I believed he felt the same toward me and would fight in my corner if I ever needed him— how gullible and wrong I was!

We lived in Dan's home for ten months. When we had to move into a smaller home, I felt immensely guilty because the children were uprooted and had to adjust to another new school and make new friends again. I did my best to ensure that the transition had a minimal effect on them but it was futile; my children loathed the interference in their lives and I detested myself for causing the disruption.

The chaos of the past two years was beginning to take a toll on me, and I started to relive parts of my childhood. I am not sure why, but I asked Mike to leave. I thought I needed time to reexamine what I wanted from life. I was confused by my inner feelings of loathing toward myself and my mistrust of men in general. I started to fear the home and any noise potentially constituted a threat. I believed I was going insane because I felt the hands of my Stepfather in the stillness of the night and screamed as he slowly exited my room, yet his footsteps were heard only by me. My bathroom had eyes watching my every move and washing with my clothes on became an obsession until I could no longer bathe at all. To me, the house was demonic as it watched me with its prying eye. Although I knew I was slipping away from reality and that my fears were self-borne, no matter how many times I tried to rationalize them, I failed with further synopses of self-loathing instead.

Making my bed in a particular way crept back into my daily routine, my need to dispel my meals returned in full force as I started bingeing and gorging food until I thought my belly would burst, then taking one-hundred plus laxatives and six heaped spoonfuls of Andrew's Liver Salts to expel the food. This behavior continued for two months until suddenly I no longer felt the urge to eat anything.

Mike was worried about me and my refusal to eat and when I had locked myself in the front room and barricaded both doors, he phoned Bobbi-Joe, desperate for help. I was lost in my own world of pain and trying to escape my abuse. My reality was too raw and I just did not care to live anymore. Bobbi was my savior that day; she spoke to me and reached a part of my soul that had buried itself within my own body. I was admitted to a psychiatric unit. It was as though I was trapped inside myself and trying to reach out but I had no strength, no emotional connection to anyone or anything. I had literally closed down and nothing could reach me—but when the nurse told me that both men and women stayed in the same units, I was terrified of being attacked at night while I slept so I was given a room of my own. I secured myself in it every night by pushing my bed against the door and shaking talc on the floor to show footprints of any intruders.

It took many weeks of therapy to understand why I had shut out reality and to talk to Mike about my abuse. Although I never saw the doctor much, I believe the solitude of my surroundings helped me understand my depression.

I met some strange and wonderful people in my cocoon of insanity. Others in the hospital were hurt and battered by life like I was. Some would walk to and fro or in a complete circle chanting to themselves. I began to heal my tortured mind and realized that I had shut down my own psyche to protect myself from any more hurt. I was luckier than most and was able to come and go as I pleased although the outside world held no attraction for me as I became more cocooned in my surroundings. For the first time, in a long time I felt safe and protected.

Eventually, I looked around myself and started to see the reality of my prison. I knew that I needed to be home with my children. Facing them was hard as they sat in the visiting room, looking at me as though I were alien to them. I was angry with myself for letting them down and regretted that they had witnessed my downfall. I could not explain to them why or how mommy got to this point in her life. I would have to explain my terrible abuse and I was *not* going to paint such ugly pictures in their young heads. The last few years had taken its toll; I was 33 years old and had experienced more in half a lifetime than many would in ten. I don't think I will ever reconcile with my lost childhood or ever forgive the people who abused me. One day, other survivors will see there is a future and light at the end of the darkest tunnel.

During this period of my life, I lost my religion and beliefs. I thought deeply about my life and the road I traveled. I also met another Molly—she was the social worker who was sent to the hospital to assess me. I was aggressive, demented and rude to her because I believed that my children would be taken from me. She was to become a dear friend whom I have the utmost respect for. I have never understood how or why, but she saw something in me that no one else apparently had.

Returning home to my children two weeks later was all the medicine I needed. We were re-housed by the local authority in a five-bedroom apartment, located in possibly the worst area I had known. Mike moved back in with us and we tried to achieve a normal existence. Within the first week of living in the apartment, there were three raids by the local police. Drug dealers, thieves and benefit fraudsters were the norm in this horrible place we now called home. I called it the ass end of the world.

My children quickly adapted and I found out that they were involved in stealing and hung out with drug dealers. Paul was courting Sue, the local drug dealer's daughter. Sue was affected emotionally by her childhood—her own father was murdered when she was small. I saw pain in her eyes when she spoke and tears hidden well in her smile. Her stepfather was now in prison due to her evidence and her mother was hell-bent on making her daughter pay. I was angered by her mother's attitude and made it clear that Sue's stepfather alone was to blame. He should never have involved a child in his illegal activities! Sue told me where her stepfather's stashes were; the largest held one hundred and eighty thousand pounds cash, the smaller ones held drugs and cash combined.

If ever my morals were tested, it was then! The thought to keep it never entered my mind until after the police were involved. I was too hyped up in a world of drug-dealing money and child abuse to realize the enormity of my involvement. Sue was taken away from the area to a place of safety and no one was told where she was until the trial was over. Her stepfather was imprisoned by her damning evidence and my own family threatened because of the relationship between her and my son. Her mother believed had she not had the support of my family, that she would never have given such damning evidence against her stepfather. Their family was in crisis long before we moved into the area.

The police informed me of their threats and intentions and installed a panic alarm within my home. I had moved to Insanity Street! I warned Sue's mother that I would take a son for a son! I was not about to hide from her or her family. During this altercation with Sue's mother, I realized the police had altered the story because they wanted to keep my family away from hers to prevent Sue from changing her statement.

Sue always turned up at my home after running away from yet another foster care placement until she was finally placed permanently with me. The relationship with her mother was to be slow to rebuild and her stepfather wrote to her to say that he no longer blamed her.

Four months later, she advised me she was pregnant and Paul my second eldest was the father. My heart ached with sadness for I knew this mixed-up child was not ready to parent another. Paul and Sue were only fifteen and sixteen years of age, too young to possibly understand the enormity of parenthood. I worried about the future and was frustrated that my first grandchild had such an unhealthy world awaiting him or her.

My sons were on the road to nowhere fast, getting involved with other local youths and breaking into buildings and stealing from the local marina. I decided we were going to move by whatever means possible. I witnessed the police goading the local youths into a confrontation and knew the attitude from any in authority was tactless when you gave the address of residence. When we eventually left the area, my perception of the people who lived there had changed. The majority were decent, honest people.

The house we moved into was in a more affluent part of town. Barrie joined the army and Paul was living with Sue and their son Joe, who was now three months old. I worried about moving so far away but needed to get away for my children's sakes. James had also decided to live on his own and moved into a flat in the same block we moved from. Gripper and Michael stayed with us and life settled once more. I was happy in our new home and decided to go back to college and study for a degree in humanities and social science—I wanted something better from life.

Mike was progressively getting weaker and returned to the doctor explaining he was unwell and falling over, his gait unsteady. His memory was also affected and he could not tolerate noise and seemed to find the simplest of things impossible to attain. He returned home with another prescription for pills and threw it on the table moaning that no one seems to understand him. He explained his body would move involuntarily; his legs jerking out, his arms trembling. He had an altered feeling down his left side and the hairs on his leg had disappeared.

As he left for work that night, I worried about his health and instinctively knew his symptoms were going to get worse long before they got better. Sometimes he was unwell for a few days, other times it would be for months. This had been going on for ten years but was definitely becoming more frequent. I desperately hoped it was not life–threatening. He returned home after only an hour, ashen-faced as he explained that he crashed the car. He had tried to apply the brake but his leg had gone into spasm instead. He was shaken and determined to go back to the doctor the following morning but when he awoke, he was unable to control the left side of his body at all and he had lost the control of his bladder—Mike was incapable of getting out of bed at all. I called the doctor who immediately admitted him to hospital. I watched as Mike was lifted into the ambulance, the worry on his face evident. Later, the doctor said he believed that Mike had suffered a stroke. I was shocked but somehow I did not think the same and asked a question I knew nothing about.

"Do you think it may be Multiple Sclerosis?"

"No, it's a stroke," the doctor assured us. An MRI and a spinal tap were ordered and we received the results a week later. He had Multiple Sclerosis. The doctor suggested that we should go home for the weekend to absorb the news. We walked from the ward in total silence as dread and desolation occupied our thoughts. All Mike knew about Multiple Sclerosis was Sir Harry Secombe's singing to raise money for others with the disease. We entered our house and I knew the life we had was lost forever as Mike stumbled through the front door, losing his footing again as if fate wanted to leave no room for hope.

Our relationship changed from man and wife to nurse and patient as the weeks rolled by and Mike's disease took hold. He seemed to gradually give in to its greedy progression and he became withdrawn and argued about the pettiest of things. He also became possessive about his personal belongings. Tools, the car, and even his model cars were off-limits to everyone—including me. I didn't know if I could continue living this way. Had Mike been this unpredictable when we first met, I surely would not have married him. I wanted my husband back and was damned if I would mourn my loss! I knew Mike was capable of achieving more but I was aware too that he had just slipped into his own depressive world.

"Pass me the cup, I'm thirsty."

I passed it to him and watched as his arms shook violently and the water cascaded over the bedding. He lost his temper and screamed about being unable to even drink and would probably be better off with a baby's bottle. I was frustrated with the scene and shouted at him to get out of bed so I could change the bedding. He seemed shocked by my reaction and a little bewildered about why I was being aggressive, but it was enough for him to saunter off toward the bathroom unaided. He crashed onto the landing and struggled to regain an upright position. I watched as he regained his control and cautiously attained his destination. It was the start of an uphill struggle that would take ten months before he achieved a reasonable level and quality of life. I was proud of the man I married and his fervor to succeed.

We learned to respect his disease but not allow it to control our lives. I resumed college and Mike accepted retirement. Things were at last starting to settle again. I watched the children closely and knew Mike's illness had affected Gripper the hardest. He seemed afraid to leave his dad alone and was always offering to help. Paul returned home when his relationship with Sue had run its course but I was concerned for Joe, my grandson. It was not long before the telltale signs of neglect appeared. Sue was struggling on her own and had started taking drugs and Paul had moved into her mother's apartment— an unhealthy arrangement in my opinion. Sue was banned from their home and her behavior became increasingly more bizarre while the relationship between her and her mother became more antagonistic. I believed they had not forgiven Sue for testifying against her stepfather and were doing all they could to see to her downfall.

I saw her stepfather differently from the way others knew him. I met him a few times when he was on home leave and could see the nasty control freak he was when his mask slipped. He was sixty years old, much older than her mother and he leaned heavily on reputation and wore the thinnest of ponytails to try to look the part. In fact, he looked like a pensioner trying to be something else. I laughed to myself when we first met. How gullible I had been. My concept of a drug dealer was a bodybuilder wearing a suit—mean, fighting machines. I was introduced to an insubstantial little old man with a grey ponytail. I looked into his eyes and smirked as I remembered the fear that rushed though me when the police had said my family was threatened by him.

But little did I know that this little weasel would do all he could to attain his goal of punishing Sue for her part in his downfall. He tried to use my grandson as a weapon against us but I ended his control by relinquishing all ties with Joe. We have held on to all correspondence connected with Joe and the circumstances causing our lack of contact. One day he will knock on my door and questions will be asked. I will be prepared, hand him all the paperwork and allow him to read the truth for himself.

The Taker of My Dreams

The taker of my dreams has no mask,
He wears his clothes as you and I.
He is a family member trusted and loved by all

The taker of my dreams has no horns,
He works hard to get what the family needs.
He is good—kind, especially to me.

The taker of my dreams wouldn't stand out in a crowd.
Just like most, he drives a car

The taker of my dreams is everyone's favorite friend.
Every neighbor would love to have this man to befriend.

The taker of my dreams is the one who would help you out,
He would baby sit—Give advice— and treat all elderly right.

The taker of my dreams is the giver of my nightmares.
He lurks in my home making every one think he cares.

The taker of my dreams is coming up the stairs.
Hello Daddy, Yes I am a good girl, take whatever is there.
Daddy is a coward, a liar, the taker of my dreams.

8 Accepting My Fate

I settled into my college classes and Mike was getting better daily but I felt tired, agitated and unable to sleep. I had pain in my belly and an uneasy feeling about my own health. I sat in the doctor's office talking to my general practitioner who had known me for a number of years. He convinced me that I was fine and that stress was responsible for my stomach pain—but I left with an uneasy feeling of dread and terror for my family and me. Any suggestion that caring for Mike was making me emotional angered me. I was going insane again with uneasy thoughts and feelings. I worried daily about slipping back to an insane world of psychological turmoil, which held me prisoner for a few months and resulted in my hospitalization. My doctor assured me that I was the sanest person he knew and that it was doubtful that I would ever have another episode again. I wished I had his ability to believe in tooth fairies and leprechauns— things just didn't *feel* right. When I asked him how many people he knew, he jokingly answered, "Maybe three." We laughed and I left feeling a little easier.

My doctor was a good man who never judged my sometimes wacky world and thoughts. He knew more about me than anyone else and I trusted this man completely. Apart from Mike and my father-in-law, there were no others. However, that was soon to change as the pain became increasingly worse and concentrating on my work in college became impossible. I was back at the doctor's office demanding to be referred to the hospital for a scan; I thought maybe I had an Ectopic pregnancy.

An appointment was made and while I lay on the bed, I watched the monitor scan my belly. Unfortunately, nothing was discovered to be amiss yet the pain increased over the weeks and eventually I was admitted into the hospital. Nothing substantial was found during examination but the doctor suggested a colonoscopy as a precaution. I had experienced constipation for years but lately, it had gotten worse. He explained the course of action to me and said that I would be sent home to prepare. I was not considered an emergency case and he added that at 36 years old, I was too young to have bowel cancer. I walked out of the hospital feeling like a scolded child, the pain still intense.

Four weeks later, I received my instructions for preparing for the procedure in the post and prepared myself for the colonoscopy scheduled to take place the following morning. After taking the medication, my insides felt like they would explode as the medicine worked its magic; it was exhausting! I inwardly laughed to myself; this stuff would have worked wonders for me a few years ago when purging on laxatives was a daily routine.

When I arrived at the hospital, a gown was thrust into my hands and I was instructed to remove all clothing, including undergarments. I was no slim babe and found the open-backed nightdress rather tight and the dressing gown was even tighter. I emerged from the changing room with my arms bent like a bodybuilder who likes to flex his muscles. I sat red-faced and hoped that my attire was not firmly stuck between my butt cheeks when called to the examination room.

I was ordered to climb onto a trolley and wheeled into an operating room. I was given a light anesthetic and my embarrassment eased; the nurses were caring and gentle. As I slowly drifted into sleep, I heard someone say 'push' so I pushed slightly and heard laughter and someone shouted, "No Mrs. Wallace. Not you!" I drifted off to sleep.

When I came around, the nurses told me the doctor had asked for the nurse to push in the colonoscope. All I heard was the word 'push' and apparently I thought he meant me—after all, I did have five children. I had forced the thing out of my butt like a bullet from a gun and surprised the doctor in the process. He had to regain his composure before he could proceed.

An appointment was made for the following week for the results of the colonoscopy. Mike and I attended together, nervous and apprehensive.

I sat and watched the doctor's mouth move but after he said *tumor* and *obstruction,* I heard nothing else. My mind spiraled as I tried to comprehend dying. I was not ready for this! The doctor pulled me back mentally when he asked if bowel cancer ran in my family. I answered, "No." I was unable to explain my past and was too shocked to enter into this conversation with him. He wanted me to return for another colonoscopy when they would try to remove the obstruction this way and avoid surgery.

During the second colonoscopy, they were unable to remove the tumor so the decision was made for me to have major bowel surgery. I was to have a sigmoid-colectomy in a few days' time. I was sent home with tablets for the pain and a morphine drip waiting at the hospital if it were needed. Mark came to visit me the night before the surgery and we avoided discussing the reason for and possible outcome of the surgery.

After the surgery, the doctor reported that the procedure had gone well and I was surprised that I felt no pain. I was a little overwhelmed by the size of the scar, but it was the price to pay for living without the physical pain. The results of the biopsy would be available in a few weeks but as long as I was eating and my bowels were working normally, I could go home.

After a few days, I noticed my tummy swelling. I was told that gas had been pumped into my belly during the operation, which was probably the cause. I told them that I had not been to the toilet since the surgery, but the nursing staff seemed fine about it and sent me home with a box of laxatives telling me that they would work in a few days. Instead, I felt steadily worse and my pain increased so rapidly I wanted to scream as I tried to pass dehydrated stools. My belly felt as though it were being twisted and turned as the pain seared through it. It was possibly the worst pain I had ever endured!

I was ultimately sent to different hospitals and referred to a variety of doctors. At my local hospital, I was given a different consultant and our first meeting was something I am sure he will never forget.

Dr. Strong received the backlash of my frustrations and lack of trust. He tried to assure me he had never come across this problem before and wanted me to speak to a counselor. I agreed to do as he asked, but was annoyed that he was making assumptions about my mental health after our first consultation. *What had the last surgeon written about me in his notes? Could he be aware of my visit to the psychiatric ward a few years ago?* If that was the reason for his insistence for a psychiatric assessment, I knew I would be having words with him.

Why do people choose to believe the perpetrator of abuse and not the victim? Why are we, the children, left to rebuild our lives after losing all when the accusations are made? Our reactions to their attitude are portrayed as unmanageable spoiled brats. Yet when it suits society, the same abuse that no-one would agree happened is then used as the excuse for the strange behavior of us adults. Ultimately, it becomes the justification for a diagnosis of psychosomatic ailments. My God, people really frustrate the hell out of me at times. However, I cannot show my frustrations, because then I am accused of being manipulative and aggressive!

I was admitted once again into the hospital with severe abdominal pain and the psychologist was asked to assess me. I was angry enough to spit nails and she was to take my aggravated attitude with grace. I sarcastically told her the pain was in my ass—not my head—and that the doctors had done something wrong. I had lived for six months with this unbearable pain and unable to go to the toilet without artificial aide. I believed the laxatives had made my bowel lazy and irreversible damage had been done.

I explained, in my usual prevailing manner, of my disgust that my past was again being used as a weapon against me. The psychologist agreed that I was as sane as she was and believed the pain was real and not psychosomatic. She recommended a scan instead.

The scan revealed a large growth on my left ovary protruding into the wall of the bowel. A total abdominal hysterectomy was recommended but I refused. I explained to the gynecologist that I wanted another child and had been trying for the past few months but the surgeon reacted as though it were a personal affront to him. I stood my ground and refused to sign the consent form until it was amended. The operation was scheduled in two weeks and I left the hospital worried if I could survive with the pain that long. What did a cyst on the ovaries have to do with the workings of the bowel, I wondered, but who was I to question the professionals, especially gynecological surgeons?

I arrived at the hospital and was prepared for surgery the following day. As I was taken to the operating theatre the next morning, I experienced a little panic as the realization that this was my second major surgery in less than a year struck home but I recovered quickly and was functioning within two days. I went home five days later and a homecare nurse was arranged to help me with my home care. She inadvertently revealed something that seemed to have been kept from me in the hospital. Her revelation altered my life and I was devastated.

When she informed me that the bleeding I was experiencing was due to a blood clot caused by my total hysterectomy, I was shocked and believed she had gotten my notes mixed-up with someone else's. After calming myself down, I realized she was not mistaken and that the operation I refused had indeed been performed anyways. I felt as though I had been abused all over again and could feel myself regressing back to the ugly feelings of my childhood—helpless, abused and worthless. I was advised to return to the hospital to get myself checked and as I walked into the building I felt as though I were falling back into the jaws of the Devil.

I came face to face with my surgeon, the one who took no heed to my choices and I surged inside with anger and wanted to physically attack this smug person smiling at me. I physically felt the angry child inside me climbing from the dark depths of my being as I once more tried to hide my feelings and speak to him as though I had nothing to hide. I was afraid to ask him, "Why?" Why did he ignore my wishes? Why did I not matter at all to him? Why did he decide I was never to have another child? Why did he think he was God? Why? Blind rage quietly coursed through me and I avoided eye contact to hide my anger.

He instructed me to lie down so he could remove my stitches while I was there but as he approached me, defensive words rolled from my mouth that I was unaware of saying. "You touch me and I will break your fucking fingers!" I snarled like a caged animal. I could not contain my anger any longer.

He carefully stepped backwards toward the door and quickly disappeared from the room. The nurse was shocked and asked what was happening? What was wrong with me?

He had opened up my body and took everything that signified me as a woman—without my permission! I was shouting and swearing hysterically at the door the surgeon had hidden behind as Mike pulled me from the room and tried to cover my mouth with his hand. I was in the deepest depths of despair as I realized it was not a dream, it had truly happened. I sobbed uncontrollably all the way home and dashed to my room, never wanting to face the world again.

My belly was empty, my pain never-ending and my life changed forever. I was 39 years old and lay on my bed sobbing like a child. Nothing Mike said could console the absolute desolation I felt. It truly was like being abused all over again. A man had waited until I was defenseless and asleep to do what he wanted to my body. As a person, a human being, I was inconsequential. I did not matter! The only thing important was the man and his desires and wishes. *I* simply did not matter! I remained in my room until the following morning and thought about my life now. I wondered how I was going to get through it all. I mourned the loss of the child I would never have and I mourned the loss of my womanhood.

The nurse informed me that I would need hormone replacement therapy (HRT) for many years, as I was still considered too young for such drastic surgery. I sat holding the patch she had given me to apply to my skin as I read the warning that using it too long can cause breast cancer. Five years is the maximum, especially if cancer was known to be a hereditary factor. I decided to contact my mother and seek out my biological father. If cancer was hereditary, my children were also at risk. I made my way downstairs and I asked Mike to pass me the phonebook because I had also decided to seek legal help—the surgeon was going to answer why he did this operation. The lawyer advised me that I had one hell of a fight on my hands and that I had signed the consent form, although I did so believing it was amended to conform to my wishes. I was not going to back down, determined that the truth would come out in the end.

I went to the police station and filed a complaint against the surgeon, claiming assault. I knew it was going to be hard to prove, I was just a common housewife but he was a well-respected surgeon. I certainly wasn't prepared for the lies I read on the many statements the police had taken, although many of the lies could be proven to be so. My perception of doctors had changed as I realized they were just ordinary people as you and I and were simply doing a job.

The power they have suddenly dawned on me. If a doctor asks you to strip, you do so even though you are not sure why you are taking off your clothes. We do so because we have been raised to believe they are to be trusted and respected. They see parts of our bodies that our partners don't even see and they are privy to our innermost fears. We usually confide in them about the most intimate things and trust their decisions to be right. My misperception has now changed and I will never trust another surgeon again. I will ask questions and seek out as much information as possible if I ever face surgery again.

I won my battle with the National Health Service despite that my own solicitor believed I did not have a chance. Lies had been told and when proven, I was made an offer to settle out of court, which I wanted to refuse. I was looking for an explanation and apology; money was never going to put anything right again, but I had to be guided by my solicitor and he wanted to accept—in his eyes we had won. In my eyes, I had been shut up! I knew the media would have probably attended and wanted my chance to warn the world about what could happen and did happen in the hospitals.

Within six months, I was back in the hospital. My body was weak with pain and my mind was close to shutting down. I had become so dependent on laxatives that I needed to take thirty daily just to get some sort of relief. I had also written to my father's sister at an old address I had kept. She had moved but the new occupants had a forwarding address. My aunt's phone call came the same day I had spoken to mother and learned that a few members of her family had bowel cancer. Talking to mother felt strange after such a long time. I replaced the receiver and felt no kinship with her.

Mike answered the phone and quickly rushed to me whispering, "It's your father's sister." I explained why I was calling and she devastated me with her answer. She had in fact just had an operation for bowel cancer and now had to have a colostomy bag. We spoke for a while and when I asked if she would forward a letter to my father, she declined explaining that he was not interested and she did not want to jeopardize her relationship with him. I was perplexed why he did not want to speak and a little angry about his attitude. I was harder in my outlook toward him now and had assigned some blame to him for what happened to me during my childhood. Had he been involved in our lives, stepfather would never have existed as part of my life and my childhood would have been different.

I emailed Dr. Strong and updated him about my condition. He immediately arranged another colonoscopy and more tumors were discovered. The last one he removed was not malignant but it would have been had it been left any longer. The doctor believed that the sheer size of it would have killed me first though. It was also decided I would have another scan and again received the medication to clear the bowel through the post to prepare myself the evening before.

My pain had become so intense I could no longer function as a normal human. I drove my car with no heed to my destination even forgetting at times how to get home. Truly forgetting for a split second where I actually lived. I would forget why I had entered a room, only to return a few times before giving up. I burnt food instead of cooking it and found my concentration waning abominably.

I knew this time was different. As the medication worked its magic, the pain I experienced ravaged my entire body and left me feeling not only exhausted but weak as well. I had waited more than an hour and still the medication had not worked. Suddenly, it happened—I could taste the most awful tang in my mouth—the smell putrid as I belched. I was horrified when I expelled my own excretion through my mouth, my throat burned and my chest heaved as again my body rampaged in reverse. I was left with terrible burning in my throat. Even though I was sure of what had just happened, I was still in shock and could not comprehend it all.

I spoke to the surgeon in the morning who advised that I should have gone straight to the hospital as it was a very dangerous thing for the body to go through. He injected blue dye into my veins and I was to lie on my stomach as a tube was inserted into my rectum and air pumped to highlight the bowel. Now I know what it would feel like to be a balloon! I heard the air rushing out of the tube into my nether region and the nurse spoke softly to me trying to alleviate my fears and humiliation as I gnawed on the sheet. She found a large obstruction, my bowel was completely obstructed by the tumor, and she would report her findings to Dr. Strong. I was shown through a door to a toilet and told to stay there and wait because the air would soon be finding its way out. I was shown a second door through which I could later finally leave.

I sat farting in a high pitch, sighing with relief as the gases churned inside. I screeched a little, yelped a little, swore a lot and sighed with relief. I was thankful this was a single toilet and

I was alone while my butt spoke in a foreign language. When the ordeal was finished, I dressed and left by the door that I had been instructed to leave by. As I opened the door, all eyes were upon me when I stepped out into the waiting area. I could have died with embarrassment and humiliation.

Mike's health was deteriorating with the stress of all we had been through, but we were able to keep the children from being aware of most of the negative things that were happening. Barrie was now living with his girlfriend and had given us a beautiful granddaughter. He was now 23 years old and Gripper, my baby, was now sixteen. I believed they had been through enough in their lives and only needed to know more if it became inevitable that I was going to die.

I entered the hospital once more but panicked when it came time to be anesthetized. Dr. Strong relayed the results of the colonoscopy straight away—many more polyps were found and because the bowel was not working, he advised that I needed a colostomy. He explained that the colostomy was a temporary measure but I was extremely apprehensive. However, I trusted this man because I had known him for a while. He helped me to overcome my fear and mistrust and I have the utmost respect for him. He was right about my operation and although I was upset about having a bag to gather my waste, I was pain free and I knew it was a temporary situation. I was up and about within 48 hours of my operation and while many others walked hunched over in pain after such an ordeal, I walked straight and upright. I had no pain or depression. I was happy and walked with a spring in my step for the first time in a long time.

Life returned to what could be considered normal and I deferred college classes for a year whilst I recovered. My children were settled and life hummed along smoothly and quietly for a while—until I received a letter from my biological father asking me to phone him.

My fingers shook as I dialed the number and then he picked up the phone. I was trembling with anticipation and hung onto his every word. I instantly reverted to being the little girl who longed for her daddy's love. We talked a little and as I replaced the receiver, Mike waited for me to convey the conversation but I burst into tears and words failed me instead. The happiness I felt was because I was finally going to meet the man I had dreamed about for most of my life and I had visions of him holding me close and explaining his absence.

Mark was weary and once more voiced his disapproval. I knew he was right; had Dad really wanted to find us, he could have used the same method I used to find him. I chose to make excuses instead because the alternative was too painful to consider.

But not to me!

The house seems full today,
  many meals have been eaten and many words spoken,
              But not to me.

It's my fifth birthday today are we gathered here for this.
All my family and friends have come together to celebrate
something.
But I might as well be invisible, they talk among
themselves
              But not to me.

Everyone is leaving wishing well to family
Kissing and hugging each other, so much love and
warmth,
              But not to me.

Mary sits chewing her nails glaring at the television.
I sit and watch her,
Mesmerized by her lack of facial expression and no
movement of eye
Mother shouts for her to turn the volume down,
Informing her dinner will be ready in ten minutes.
              But not to me.

Johnny runs into the room and takes a flying leap onto the
sofa
I jump with him.
Father calls for him to stop.
              But not to me.

Bono runs into the lounge, chasing his ball, knocking over
the coffee table.
He stops and stares at me, making a whimpered exit from
the room,

Thankful he responds to me, I am beginning to think no
one cares—he runs from me.

Mother shouts for all to join her in the dining room
Everyone scrambles to the table—including me.
All have their places set,
 I run around twice searching my little space
Mother yells for everyone to sit.
                              But not to me.

I find my place, but there is no food on my plate,
No drink in my cup.
Standing against the wall, I try to make sense of the
strangeness around me.
They look to each other.
                              But not to me.

I watch as they start to eat and there is an eerie silence in
the room.
Mother toys gently with her food, Father pushes his plate
away.
He cups his head in his hands, and starts to sob,
Mother rushes to his side and through his sobs he says
how sorry he is
Addressing the whole family he apologizes to all.
                              But not to me.

Mother reaches for the family photo from the mantle,
Caressing her fingers gently over the picture.
In a soft pure voice she whispers to father
        "It was not your fault—she will understand"
I lean over mothers shoulder to glimpse the picture,
It shows a happy family
Her tears fall on the glass frame and I wrap my arms
around her tight.
I love her scented smell—She speaks again to father.
                              But not to me.

Grandma and Grandpa walk into the room hand in hand
They gesture for me to join them
 They speak only to me

I am sad to leave my family my home
I want to tell father he was not to blame.
The car skidded the fire was not his fault,
He tried all he could he managed to get to everyone in
time.
 But not to me.

I am at peace happy to be able to see them all one last time
Mother and father are still talking only they talk about me
 But not to me.

9 Onwards and Upwards

I had been calling my father weekly for a month when he finally announced that he would be visiting Devon in three months. I was anxious and afraid that he might not like me because I was overweight. I feared he would be disappointed when he saw me. Most of all, I needed to tell him about my childhood and let him know, perhaps to warn him, that I had written about the abuse and other past experiences and hoped to eventually have it published. I decided it best to tell him on the phone before he arrived so I dialed his number and held my breath as the phone shrilled its chorus. Dad answered the phone and I asked that he listen to what I had to say. I knew I could not do this face to face because if he showed any disgust toward me it would have destroyed me. After I had finished, he assured me the only people responsible were my Mother and Stepfather. I did not tell him that I also blamed him because had he been involved in my life, I believe the abuse would never have happened—or I would have had someone to turn to at least.

Mother was still in contact with me but by now our relationship had changed. Maybe it was because she was older and alone, who knows? We were closer than we had ever been. Mother started to open up about her life with my biological father and the reasons for their divorce. She said he was a womanizer who left mother alone while he had his affairs. They had lived in Army quarters and mother found it hard to cope with three young babies and a husband who was never around.

He left one morning and never returned, which caused the loss of our home and mother had no choice but to place her three babies into care. It was 1959 and there was no welfare or social security that would help. I believe mother became mentally ill with the strain of her past that was never acknowledged and she was never helped and could never recover. She was now showing signs of Alzheimer's disease and was doing odd things; her short-term memory had started to fail and she was beginning to rely on me for the most menial of tasks. I resented her neediness and questioned myself for helping her.

We talked about my father and his family. She was finally eager to answer anything I asked—how I wish she had been this way when I was younger. We talked about her second husband and the vile abuse he dished out to all her children. She now showed remorse but I was never truly convinced it was genuine. She always tried to sell me on how hard she was abused by her second husband: the beatings she endured to protect her children. Her supposed self-sacrifice only made me angrier. *Why did she stay with him if he abused her so badly? Why did she allow him to abuse her children?* I have to add that I never saw her beaten by him, but then no one saw Stepfather abusing me either.

The conversation inevitably led to discussions of my stepfather sexually abusing me and the atmosphere became tense between us as she explained why she chose to turn a blind eye. Mother tried explaining that she had an idea something was wrong, she had felt him returning to her bed at night and knew he had just come from my bedroom. When she questioned him, he told her she was "a nasty old bag for even thinking he could hurt me that way."

He constantly spat at her to "take her batty pills" for her nasty thoughts. I remembered him using these words to her at times. Mother was made to feel guilty but, her suspicions never completely yielded. Mother explained she disbelieved my allegations the same way she was brainwashed into believing she also was wrong. She only realized the truth when I handed her two letters. I had forgotten about them. I handed them to her in anger when mother had asked me many years before if I spoke the truth. I outlined on paper and in detail, the night devil's abuse. I taunted them to take me to court for slander if I were lying and I signed the letter for them. I repeated the same about mother and detailed her abuse toward me, inviting her to confront her husband and myself together if needed. Neither of them approached me.

I was never sure if the night devil received my letter, only that mother divorced him soon after and phoned me asking that I make a statement to her solicitor about my horrific abuse at the hands of her husband. I declined, unsure whether Mother was in fact married to him. We never saw photographs of a wedding and I had been the victim of her many mind games in the past. No way was she going to use my childhood to gain her freedom when she was just as guilty as he. It was through this phase of our relationship that mother seemed to decline in her mental state and I often wonder if speaking so frankly to me was the catalyst for her demise.

I decided to visit father's home because I was incapable of waiting three months. Mother warned me not to allow him to hurt me which I found rather bizarre coming from the parent who had hurt me beyond words.

The drive was long and sticky as the sun shone bright in the summer sky. We pulled up outside his home and I could not believe I was actually here. I rang the doorbell and a man answered but I did not have to question if he were my dad because it was as though my oldest brother was standing there—the resemblance was uncanny and a little upsetting. He embraced me and I savored being in the arms of my dad. We were invited in and as I walked into his home I felt a little angry. This man was not poor and certainly not ill. I wondered what excuse he would give for not including his children in his life. As I was shown around his home, there were many similarities to my own.

Mother lived in squalor and never had anything worth giving away yet my home was always neat and clean. I had always wondered whom I took after more and it was obvious—I was an Arscott. I had an uncanny feeling of belonging. I sat outside smoking a cigarette and wanting to pinch myself; I was actually sitting on my father's doorstep. A hand brushed me gently across the head and I looked up to see it was my father who stroked me so tenderly; he smiled. He led me to his garage and held the door open for me. I was happy that I was able to walk into this building with this stranger and feel no threat emanating from him.

I teased him about his treasures and we shared a moment together that will always be special as he hugged me close and for an instant there was only my dad and me in the world and it was free of any pain. For a few minutes I was a little girl experiencing the closeness, protection and love that a daughter normally feels with a loving father, for the first time. We talked for many hours that night but once my father retired to bed his wife explained that everything in the home was hers and had belonged to her before they married. She did not know my father had already explained that he had purchased most of the home. I ignored her remarks that we were too old to have a father and daughter relationship and that maybe we should settle for a friendship. I was quick with my reply; I already had many friends but he was my father—whether I was one or one hundred and one years of age! Biologically, that was a fact, I smugly stated.

I was angry with her. She had nothing that I wanted, apart from a relationship with my father. I hid a lot of my feelings and resisted asking him why he turned his back on his own bloodline yet could raise other women's children.

As we left his home the following day to return to ours, I was glad I had made the effort for this visit and believed father was as excited as I was and that he was ready to make a real effort too.

Two months later, he came to Devon with his wife but they refused to stay in my home and chose to stay at a hotel instead. Mother found it tormenting to know I had been to visit my father and that he was coming to my home. My children did not make much fuss about the visit. Maybe they saw something that I didn't but they were happy because I was happy. The visit went well but it was starting to feel false, there was no warmth in their smiles and their words seemed rehearsed. We were invited to my father's seventieth birthday party later in the year but Mark refused to attend and Paul, our oldest brother flatly refused to even meet him. I'm sure Paul remembers things from his childhood, his own personal nightmares that he refuses to share with his siblings.

Once again we made the journey to father's home, this time to celebrate his birthday but when we arrived, we were informed we had to stay in a hotel. His wife's children were visiting and they had little ones so their three spare bedrooms were all going to be occupied. We were a little disappointed with their inhospitality but we checked in to a local hotel and waited for the evening. I was starting to feel awkward and a little rejected. We arrived at the house and were introduced to my father's neighbors and friends and we also met his wife's children who informed us they were not staying at the house at all, but instead had planned to return home after the party as had been arranged weeks before. I was upset and walked into the garden to hide my tears. I did not understand why my father was reacting like this—he had been fine when we first met. I was totally dumbfounded why he was now treating me this way.

Mike did not like the way it was going and cautiously mentioned that I was the only one trying but I snapped at him that he was wrong. I knew a parent was rejecting me again and my self-worth was damaged so it was easier for me to pretend than to face the truth. How could I return home and tell Mark, Paul and mother that they were all right and father is a coward. I was desperate for it to work, but I could see his wife was the instigator. She saw me as a threat. I was his only daughter and she believed her children would be neglected if the relationship between my father and I progressed. I was hurt and frustrated— didn't she realize I needed only my father and nothing materialistic from them? Apparently materialistic people consider all others as materialistic too, so she would always think of me as competition.

I phoned him nearly every week, but he never returned my calls. I was devastated and hurt beyond description. My good friend Maria helped me put everything into proper perspective. She said she would have been proud to have me for a daughter. But the pain and emotional turmoil of rejection will always be with me. It's difficult to overcome and believe anyone can love you if your own parents do not love you. I have shed more tears than I ever thought possible and people don't understand the loss I felt when my father came into my life. I wonder why he ever asked me to phone him in his initial letter; maybe it would have been better if he remained an enigma. Maybe he wanted to appease his own curiosity at my expense. He is a coward and I was naive enough to believe he wanted a healthy, loving, father-daughter relationship. I never relayed the truth to mother and to this day she believes I am still in contact with my father.

I was due to go to the hospital for another examination and hopefully a reversal of my colostomy but my results were not good; a permanent Ileostomy was necessary. I accepted my fate and considered living pain free to be more important. I watch my children with their children and know I ended the dysfunctional lineage that had been passed down through generations of abusers. My grandchildren are to be cherished and future generations after them.

I entered the hospital with pride and a feeling of success because I knew I had raised my children the right way despite that the odds were stacked against us. My children will remember me with warm fondness and memories that will bring joy to their hearts. Even though I had lost faith in the existence of a higher entity, deep in my soul I wanted to believe I was wrong. I put my life in the hands of God and closed my eyes once again while Dr. Strong performed his magic. I awoke from my operation with mixed emotions; happy to be able to get on with the rest of my life, but depressed with the end results of my journey. I developed an allergy to the glue used on the Ileostomy bags and became very sore. The next few months were taken up with doctor's visits and stoma care as my body seemed allergic to every glue ever made.

Mike's health had been good for many months and his walking improved. I, on the other hand, seemed to be getting worse; my bones ached and my memory became muddled at times. I was gaining weight at an alarming rate and my patience became nonexistent but I stifled my intolerance when my grandchildren visited and the house resembled a war zone from their sticky fingers and droppings of food. Lauren, my oldest granddaughter, was aware of my bag and I was always open and honest with her when she asks questions.

Mike insisted I go to the local Do It Yourself shop with him. I had shied away from public places for fear of my bag leaking or someone bumping into me in a supermarket and causing it to burst. I went directly to the toilets to empty it as soon as we arrived so I could walk around with ease. I heard someone enter the room and could make out a child's voice. I finished what I was doing and opened the cubicle door and made my way to the sinks. The child looked at me with curiosity in her eyes and the adult stared as though I were an alien. They left and I looked about my person expecting to find spillage on my clothing or something, but could find nothing amiss so I headed back out to join Mike. I noticed the lady from the toilet talking to a man and obviously pointing at me. I was getting agitated and a little perplexed—*what I had done?* The man approached us and said that I should use the men's toilets and that he considered people like me to be disgusting.

Was I being set up for some sort of television show? I didn't see any cameras and I waited for him to laugh; but he was serious. I was astounded! *What the hell was he saying?* Mike then told me that he had overheard their conversation when the wife and child had exited the toilet. The child had looked under the partition between the toilets and saw me standing to urinate; they believed I was a transvestite. I didn't know if I should laugh or cry as I stared in total disbelief but I was not willing to explain why I was standing to these nosy people. Anger then swept over me and I shouted that the child should not be allowed to peek at others in a toilet and there was a law against assholes like him and that I was more woman than his wife.

They scurried away quickly as I shouted obscenities after them. Mike calmed me down and I sat on bags of sand trying to regain my composure.

"Welcome back, Shaz!" Mike laughed.

"What are you going on about Mike? I want to go and scream at them more! What's wrong with me?" I questioned.

"You just woke up." He wrapped his arm around me and we made our way back to the car without buying anything. Mike was right. I had allowed myself to slip into depression and it was controlling my life.

We sat in the car in the car park and talked for hours. I opened up with complete honesty. I cried for my body and the way it now looked. I laughed about the scene in the toilet and cried again as I poured out my heart about my life and the many obstacles I had to face and overcome. The good thing to emerge from my childhood is realizing that we don't have to repeat history and that we don't have to own the misery of our childhoods. We can refuse it and return it to its rightful owner— the abuser. A child reacts to a situation; the situation does not react to a child. I was able to leave and heal and become the child I never was and the parent they would never be.

I was lucky to have a man like Mike who cherished me and taught me how to love unconditionally. My life could have been very different. We finally made our way home after staying and talking in the car park for four hours. I entered my home stronger and more determined than ever.

The following morning I sat at my desk, booted up my computer and began to write about my life. I lived in a house full of whispers and secrets as a teenager and I am the survivor of others rages and demons. I decided to call the book *A House Full of Whispers*. The first in a trilogy—I wonder if it will ever be finished?

Why, How, When?

Floating on by in emotional pools,
evil in the air, lies confuse.
A Man who taunts, making nightmares stay,
those who keep all his secrets at bay
I ask for someone to tell the truth
to stand by me to help regain my youth.

But everyone thinks of only themselves afraid to offend,
so they sit on the fence.
Children hide feelings of shame and regret
many don't say when they feel the threats.
People in glass houses shouldn't throw stones
people who know the evil that has been done.

Why keep quiet and watch the plight
of the innocent children tortured at night?
Why not speak out, cry for what has been done?
Why not stand and be counted rebuke, not shun?

Don't agree and smile call the lost souls liars,
don't let evil he spawns become his desires.
Why don't the humans speak out and be heard,
what makes them afraid to be estranged from the herd?
Why allow the images to be called a lie,
when tears that fall make them want to die?

Evil has spawned, wrongdoing has been born,
a life sentence for the child who will be ignored.
Adults have the power to stop a wrongdoing man,
but most choose to ignore and so the evil can spawn.

He laughs at the people, the ones who ignore,
he looks for another victim maybe at their own door
But one day he will strike and the victim will be heard,
and the evil man will be castrated and stopped from causing
more hurt.

Epilogue

My mother is back in my life and dependent on me for her daily living. She became more mentally unbalanced and needed me in an emotional capacity as well. People often ask me, "Why do you so much for her when she treated you badly?" The only answer I can give is that I am not a vindictive person by nature. I will never forgive the people who abused me and one day my stepfather will be held accountable for the crimes he committed against me. He was a bully and a coward who used my childhood and vulnerability for his own perverted pleasure. My story is far from over, however! The next seven years would test my ability as a mother and my stance as a daughter. I began to realize how many survivors of abuse within the home are living under a dark shroud of secrecy, afraid to come forward to expose who and what have hurt them.

The law protects the animal's identity who stole my childhood, until he decides to expose himself to the world. I know he won't do this because he would be opening Pandora's Box. I believe that both parties should be subjected to a lie detector test. I am all for this and it's my belief that anyone who declines must be worried about the results. I have heard the arguments that it's an infringement on their human rights, but so would be false allegations. Surely it would be better to prove a liar than to live with the stigma of false contention.

I would also do what most parents fear most and fight for my sons' survival against the evils of this modern society in which we live. Nothing I had gone through in my life could compare with the devastation and terror I would face with him and nothing could rival my instincts to fight whoever stood in my way. In the coming years, I would fight for him to beat the Devil's whore: heroin addiction.

www.ingramcontent.com/pod-product-compliance
Lightning Source LLC
Chambersburg PA
CBHW032101080426
42733CB00006B/368

* 9 7 8 1 9 3 2 6 9 0 9 0 3 *